# WHAT'S SO FUNNY?

# WHAT'S SO FUNNY?

## A ROAD MAP TO HUMOUR IN DANGEROUS TIMES

Mira Falardeau

Library and Archives Canada Cataloguing in Publication

Title: What's so funny? : a new road map to humour in dangerous times / Mira Falardeau.
Other titles: Humour et liberté d'expression. English
Names: Falardeau, Mira, 1948- author
Description: Translation of: Humour et liberté d'expression: les langages de l'humour. | Includes bibliographical references and index.

Identifiers: Canadiana (print) 20240441796 | Canadiana (ebook) 20240441834 | ISBN 9781771618120 (softcover) | ISBN 9781771618137 (PDF) | ISBN 9781771618144 (EPUB) | ISBN 9781771618151 (Kindle)

Subjects: LCSH: Wit and humor, Pictorial. | LCSH: Wit and humor—History and criticism. | LCSH: Picture interpretation. | LCSH: Caricatures and cartoons—Technique. | LCSH: Freedom of expression. | LCSH: Freedom of speech. | LCSH: Discourse analysis, Literary.
Classification: LCC NC1320.F3413 2024 | DDC 809.7—dc23

All rights reserved. Without limiting the rights under copyright reserved here, no part of this publication may be reproduced, stored in or introduced into any retrieval system, or transmitted in any form or by any means—electronic, mechanical, by photocopy, recording or otherwise—without the prior written permission and consent of both the copyright owners and the Publisher of this book.

Published by Mosaic Press, Oakville, Ontario, Canada, 2025.
MOSAIC PRESS, Publishers
www.Mosaic-Press.com
Copyright © Mira Falardeau, 2025

Cover Illustration: André-Philippe Côté, *Le Soleil*, 2019
Cover Design: Amy Land
The unsigned drawings (onomatopoeia, manga illustrations, icons) are from the author.
This book is an updated and adapted translation of *Humour et liberté d'expression, Les langages de l'humour*, published in 2015 by Les Presses de l'Université Laval, Quebec

Printed and bound in Canada.

**MOSAIC PRESS**
1252 Speers Road, Units 1 & 2, Oakville, Ontario, L6L 2X4
(905) 825-2130 • info@mosaic-press.com • www.mosaic-press.com

# THANKS

For collaborating on the English version, thanks to Glenn Gavin.
Thank you to all of the cartoonists who gracefully agreed to give me the right to reproduce their drawings.

# ALSO BY MIRA FALARDEAU

*A History of Women Cartoonists*, Mosaic Press, 2020
*L'art de la bande dessinée actuelle au Québec*, Presses de l'Université Laval
  (PUL), 2020
*Humour et liberté d'expression. Les langages de l'humour*, PUL, 2015
*Femmes et humour*, PUL, 2014
*Histoire de la caricature au Québec* with Robert Aird, VLB éditeur, 2009
*Histoire de la bande dessinée au Québec*, VLB éditeur, 2008
*Histoire du cinéma d'animation au Québec*, VLB éditeur, 2006
*La bande dessinée au Québec*, Le Boréal Express, 1996

# TABLE OF CONTENTS

| | |
|---|---|
| **Introduction** | xi |
| **Chapter 1: The Birth of Comic Language** | 1 |
| The Birth of Ancient Comedy in Greece | 2 |
| The First Comic Graffiti | 6 |
| The Medieval Comic | 8 |
| The Renaissance | 10 |
| **Chapter 2: Exaggeration** | 18 |
| **Chapter 3: Simplification** | 30 |
| **Chapter 4: Simplification/Exaggeration** | 40 |
| Ideograms | 47 |
| Stereotypes | 50 |
| Parody and Mediatization of Humour | 54 |
| Cancel Culture and Humour | 57 |
| **Chapter 5: Contrast** | 59 |
| Irony or Saying the Opposite | 64 |
| **Chapter 6: Inversion** | 68 |
| **Chapter 7: Repetition, Accumulation, Gradation** | 78 |
| Accumulation | 81 |
| Gradation | 84 |
| **Chapter 8: Transfers-Anthropomorphism** | 88 |
| Mechanization of Movement | 99 |

**Chapter 9: Word and Image Games**     103

    The Pun     103

    Other Word Games     105

    Double Meaning     107

    The Visual Pun     110

    Visual Double Meaning     112

**Chapter 10: Nonsense and Snapshot**     114

**Chapter 11: Metaphor and Metonymy**     122

    Visual Metaphor     126

    Visual Metonymy     136

    The Globalization of Humour     145

**Conclusion**     153

**Bibliography**     159

**Index**     165

It is better to laugh, than to write tears,
For laughter is unique to humanity.

— François Rabelais, *Gargantua*

# INTRODUCTION

Humour is everywhere and nowhere. It is not a subject in itself but rather a way of seeing life. Humour is deeply human yet so difficult to describe. Everybody has had this troubling experience: you are sitting in a movie theater and suddenly, you burst into laughter at a funny scene while your neighbor remains stone-faced. Or the opposite. In short, not everyone laughs at the same things. However, everyone experiences pleasure while laughing.

Humour is this state of mind that consists of presenting reality in a ridiculous or absurd way by means of words, images, gestures, or mimicry. The language of humour follows a fairly constant pattern, and it is this path that I intend to examine in order to understand the mechanisms that result in humour. The processes are relatively simple, and we can observe their effects in everyday life.

Indeed, the laughable is all around us – in daily life, on a street corner, in a school yard, at the back of a classroom. The classroom is very often where most of us had our first intense laughter, the kind that does not stop, that brings on tears, hiccupping, panting, and a feeling of being wonderfully relaxed. Because laughter is good for us, it is restful, it relaxes and predisposes to openness. This sort of laughter, unpredictable and spontaneous, is not the kind that will be the center of attention here. And by the way, isn't that kind of humour what we call comical? Humour as understood here is intentional, it is a critical and corrosive state of mind. But again, this is a slippery slope, as the terms describing humour overlap with one another.

The current practice of using the term "humour" in all situations is probably a passing trend. It is staggering to see the multiple uses of this concept in our leisure society, also called the "humor-

## WHAT'S SO FUNNY?

ous society" by Lipovetsky in *The Ephemeral Era* (1983), that says it all! **What interests me here is the approach of committed humour, the critical humour that accompanies freedom of speech.** Besides, isn't one of the primary functions of humour to make people think while laughing, and not just to make people laugh? *"Castigat ridendo mores"* — Mores critically examined through laughter — according to this ancient Roman proverb defining the function of the comic playwright.

This phrase learned in a college Latin class has always made me dream: yes, to make people laugh but with a goal, that goal being to improve ourselves and improve the human condition, to become a little more human in fact, since laughter is unique to humankind, according to the maxim of Rabelais.

Everyone knows that there is no foolproof recipe for humour. The question is not why we laugh. Or how we laugh. Or the benefits of laughter. These questions could be left to philosophers and psychologists. Here I will only be looking at what it is that makes us laugh. What are the processes that have been used by cartoonists and humourists since the dawn of time to make us laugh and think in the meantime?

These processes overlap and repeat themselves in all types of combinations. To identify each process, I will present examples from the classics, texts or images, often citing pioneers of each of these art forms. Greece, Rome, Europe, the United States, Japan and finally Canada and Quebec will be the main sources of examples. How were the examples chosen? The primary goal of each author had to be to make people laugh in order to make them think. The texts are those of fables and comic songs, comic monologues, short stories or humorous writings. The images are mainly from comics and cartoons. Concerning the mix of visual and verbal humour, forms of expression are multiple: they range from burlesque theater to comedy, from comic cinema to animation cinema, from humorous comics to comic videos on YouTube or other websites, including animated caricatures and multiple satirical websites and blogs. When it is possible, I will give preference to examples from the work of women artists.

Comic advertising is not covered, although a large proportion of prize-winning advertisements use comic methods. Laughter in advertising is used to attract the attention of the public in order to sell. This seems very different from – if not the opposite of – the noblest function of committed humour, namely, to stimulate critical thinking.

## MIRA FALARDEAU

Works performed specifically for children are also excluded, although the concept of requiring childhood gathering momentum from the beginning — specific cultural works is relatively recent. The candor and naivety of such works place them in a separate category.

We will see the development of the humorous processes through the prism of the most popular figures of style: **simplification, exaggeration,** the mix thereof, then **contrast, inversion** and **repetition**. After that, we will change levels of reality and are going to see transfers between two levels, first between human forms and animal forms (**anthropomorphism**), then between human forms and object forms (**mechanization**), then **word and image games, nonsense,** and, finally, more subtle processes such as transfers between two actions, as in **metaphor** and **metonymy**. Here is, in short, the most current vocabulary of humour.

Here is the profile of every chapter. After a brief definition of each comic process, often including the description of that mechanism in real life, apart from the act of creation, we will invite readers to see that process in action with examples, texts or images, drawn from the occidental artistic heritage. This panorama will always fellow a chronological path, ending logically with contemporary examples. Each example will be analysed in its form and its content, underlining its particularities. The final project will be to show pathways of human imagination in denouncing stupidity or malice through the angle of humour.

It is obvious that different techniques can be found simultaneously in various elements of language. **In text**: we speak of words, of the structure of sentences, of presentation of situations, and of the structure of narration. **In visual discourse**: in lines and forms, facial expressions, gestures, movement, and action. And in the case of works built on both components – verbal and visual – we are faced with a vast array of techniques! Whether in theater, cinema, animated cinema, comics, and to a lesser degree in comic monologue and caricature with text, the processes interact with each other. Except for the first chapter spanning more than a thousand years, we have chosen a presentation that is rather a journey through the various methods of humour than a strict historical development. This allows us to penetrate the secrets of creators and to feel like accomplices in all the intricacies of freedom of expression.

xiii

CHAPTER 1

# THE BIRTH OF COMIC LANGUAGE

When and how was humorous language born? Since time immemorial, humans have laughed and have spontaneously been tempted to reproduce comic figures in their artworks and in their stories. The Phoenicians installed grotesque figures on the prows of their ships to repel enemies, around the 13th century BCE, in present-day Lebanon (Alexandre, 1892). Traces of these grimacing creatures are found in all primitive arts, on terracotta or wood figurines, or statuettes in more noble materials such as ivory or stone, exhibiting their hideous, buffoonish forms of small familiar gods intended either to accompany rites or to protect and ward off misfortune. Whatever the cult, these little gods, sometimes affected by a funny infirmity or defect, say comic words that can be deciphered on the walls of temples or on sacred objects like vases or amphorae. For example, the dwarf god Bes, from Sudan, found in ancient Egypt's 12th dynasty (17th and 18th centuries BCE): this rascal is always hilarious and drives out evil spirits.

We can begin to speak of true humorous language in ancient Greece, speech genuinely intended to make people laugh for the purpose of criticizing. Two visions about the emergence of comic creation clash. The first, which is our position, argues it has always existed, seeing critical humour as a fundamental activity of the human mind. The second, cautiously, does not recognize the appearance of comedy and caricature until the 17th century.

## WHAT'S SO FUNNY?

Proponents of the second view claim the omnipresence of religion in the arts prevents pieces created before the 17th century from being viewed in the same way as subsequent ones. These analysts display a certain reserve in treating ancient works on the same basis as those produced since the Renaissance. "The Satyrs of Antiquity, the *Polichilelles* of the Italian comedy, the funny figures and the gargoyles of Gothic architecture belong to a category of phenomena which are constantly changing in meaning" (Hoffmann,1958). These scholars maintain humour and religion have always been incompatible. In a way, they are not wrong. Before modern times, one could not openly laugh at a political leader, since this would be disrespecting the divinity. Indeed, temporal power and divine power were always superimposed until the age of revolutions. They still are in some cultures. This explains why current religious heads of states can imprison or, worse, mutilate cartoonists under the pretext the latter dared to make fun of them. Which amounts, they claim, to making fun of the very divinity. For example, in 2011, the Syrian cartoonist Ali Ferzat had both hands broken as a "warning" because he dared to make fun of Syrian President Bashar al-Assad, drawing him hitchhiking in the company of Colonel Gaddafi.

However, to people's delight, over the centuries, civilizations have developed strategies to circumvent such prohibition. A stroll through early recorded comic speech takes us into ambiguous territory where mockery is tolerated within certain limits. Even if a direct attack on a leader is unthinkable as is criticism of the power structure, subtle ways were found very early on of getting around this ban. We will concentrate on a certain number of these subterfuges.

## The Birth of Ancient Comedy in Greece

Upon the birth of democracy in ancient Greece, comedy was tolerated insofar as it did not upset the established order and took into account the accepted social hierarchy, and found inspiration, directly or indirectly, in the rites performed in deference to the deities. What about the combination of comedy, religion, and salacity? Now, let us note that the association between these three realms is as old as the emergence of humour itself. We must obviously distinguish between appearances of the comic integrated into ritual processes as in Archaic Greece (circa 800–500 BCE) and the later manifestations of mockery turned against cults and their officiants in Classical Greece (circa 500–300 BCE).

## MIRA FALARDEAU

In Archaic Greece, in *The Iliad* and *The Odyssey*, attributed to the poet Homer (7th century BCE), we laugh with the gods and not against them. Ritual laughter not only obeys strict codes, but above all, can only be expressed at certain times of the year. There is a time for Dionysian outbursts just as there is a time for the ensuing carnivals. When the holidays are over, everyone goes home and life goes on; in order and according to the rules.

A very widespread myth — but erased from schoolbooks to preserve the innocence of young consciences — refers to the laughter of Demeter (Ballabriga, 2006), goddess of earth and harvest. The poor goddess, devastated by having lost her daughter Persephone, kidnapped by Hades, is so sad that she is always crying and no longer eating. Old Baubô will make her laugh by lifting her skirts and waddling. She shows her bum and then her genitals to Demeter playing with these parts to give them crazy shapes. Demeter, cramped by laughter, agrees to feed herself; then, the earth becomes fertile again. A similar story takes place in the Japanese cult of the goddess Amaterasu (Feuerhmahn, 2000) where *Ame no mikoto*, a female kami, performs a saucy dance where she shows the tips of her breasts and her vulva, causing general hilarity.

We see the same salacity in rituals. One of the funniest rites concerns the Thesmophories, feasts reserved in Greece for female citizens, initiated in Eleusis. They were invited to express themselves in vulgar language, customary in brothels. The priestesses even whispered in their ears that they should commit adultery, and women replied with raw mockery. In short, a great catharsis! Ballagrida has found the same outlet in a ritual in Zambia, Africa, among the Ndembu, where wives harangue their husbands bragging about having secret lovers, all in a very mocking tone. The ultimate goal of these outbursts is to gain control over one's own impulses by first leaning towards excess permitted by ritual obscenities through comedic speech.

The same catharsis takes place in the Dionysian festivals celebrated in ancient Greece at the end of December or the beginning of January, where Dionysus, the god of wine and theater, is worshiped, mounted on a float. Silenus, a lewd drunkard, accompanied by grimacing satyrs forming a set of grotesque masked creatures, drunk and endowed with false erect sexes, is driven through the streets of the cities to the presentation sites. Their disturbing libations punctuated by buffoon songs end with a comedy or a tragedy, or both. The origins of these festivities (Minois, 2000) can be traced back to fields

# WHAT'S SO FUNNY?

in Dionysia where masked peasants, sometimes disguised as women, walked in processions in the streets, exhibiting a giant phallus as a symbol of fertility.

To end the party, they drank to the point of intoxication, singing obscene songs and cursing the audience, or *kômos*. From this *kômodia* arose the concept of comedy. Thus, making fun of others was associated with laughter in these moments of exaltation also evoked chaos, the upheaval of social order. To reinforce these excesses, at the end of the comedies, the chorus would sometimes leave the stage, generating a deafening cacophony to illustrate the chaos. We find these same excesses in carnivals and staged hullaballoos, traces of which remain in our time.

Usually, the rise of democracy is ascribed to Greece around the 5th century BCE. The birth of democracy and the notion of humour necessarily go hand in hand because democratic thought calls for discussion and the confrontation of ideas. Obviously, the reverse is easy to see nowadays in the many dictatorships which proscribe caricature as a weapon of protest.

Aristophanes (446–386 BCE) synthesized all these excesses as we can see in his plays which have come down to us. "Aristophanes' devastating laughter leaves nothing standing; sacred and profane sink pell-mell into ridiculousness, as well as the crudest obscene there is. Unbridled sexuality, scatology, [...]" argues Minois (2000). Aristophanes therefore leads the parade with his highly provocative comedies. Even though he signed his first three plays with a pseudonym, he was threatened with trial from the start and continued to fight throughout his career. Of the 44 plays this corrosive playwright is supposed to have created, only 11 have survived. In *The Clouds* (423 BCE), he mocks Socrates, in *The Wasps* (422 BCE), courts and judges, in *The Birds* (414 BCE) he laughs at politics, which he continues to mock in *The Assemblywomen* (392 BCE) and *The Frogs* (405 BCE). In short, Aristophanes' plays not only ridiculed mores but also politicians and the management of the city through allusions and metaphors easily understood by his contemporaries. Rome reproduced, with Plautus (254–184 BCE) and Terence (185–160 BCE), the same type of allegorical mockery.

The Greek physician Hippocrates (460–370 BCE) developed the theory of the four humours and his successor Galen (131–201) deduced from it the concept of the four temperaments: the choleric (yellow or red bile), the sanguine (blood), the phlegmatic (*pituita*) and the melancholic (black bile). The philosopher Aristotle (384–322 BCE) himself approved Hippocrates' ideas in *First Analytics*, 350 BC.

Aristotle spoke of comedy in these clairvoyant terms: "The comic consists of a defect or ugliness" (*Poetics*, Chap. 5). This is the winning recipe of ancient comedies: criticizing individual and social behavior as if everyone was more or less involved. The stereotypes were then built with such vividness that they have remained in our collective imagination.

I. Actor holding his two masks, 5th century BCE ("Masters of Olympus" exhibition in Quebec's Museum of Civilization, 2015).

It should be noted that few actors were used, only 3 or 4 per play, each performing many roles, from that of slave to that of prince or princess, as we could see in this exhibition "Masters of Olympus"! All they had to do was to change their mask! Indeed, no woman was allowed to play in the theater and this ban continued until the Elizabethan era — 16th and 17th centuries. In Athenian and, later, Roman comedy, with happy combinations of profane and sacred, joyfully marrying popular farce and political allusions, we witness several

## WHAT'S SO FUNNY?

levels of discourse. If someone points out defects, they are not of a particular individual, but rather of society as a whole. "Castigat ridendo mores" says the Latin proverb. Yes, we can try to correct mores by laughing. The scenes are earthy, full of misunderstandings and absurd situations. Reading this rich collection of ridiculous situations gives the impression of already witnessing the emergence of most of the comic canvases before they spread throughout the Middle Ages and the commedia dell'arte until the neo-classical era. We find the eternal conflicts between various social groups, young people against old, women against men. When Aristophanes, in *The Assemblywomen* (the play is, as one can guess, about women deciding to sit in the Assembly with men), makes the fifth woman say: "I started by throwing the razor out of the house, in order to become all hairy and no longer look like a woman at all", inevitably, the image of this hairy woman springs to our mind and our first instinct is to laugh. Herein lies the principle of inversion, where we laugh at a woman who looks like a man, as well as the other way around! These sassy women also decide to go on a sex strike to encourage their men to think! What freshness and what modernity!

### The First Comic Graffiti

The first known humorous graffiti was found on a wall in Pompeii (Melot, 1975). Another very ancient one, found on a wall of the *domus Gelotiana* on the Palatine Hill, is now exhibited at the Palatine Museum in Rome.

II. Anon., *Rufus*, Pompeii, 1st century.

# MIRA FALARDEAU

III. Anon., "*The Alexamenos graffito*" also known as *Blasphemous graffito*, "*Alexamenos cebete theon*" (Alexamenos worships (his) God), Palatine Museum, Palatine Hill, Rome, circa 1st and 3rd century.

In the first one, a specific individual's name, Rufus, is traced in lime. It is therefore really the first known caricature the deadly lava spill from Vesuvius on the wonderful city of Pompeii in 79 left intact, on a rather hazardous support, a wall. The second was also found on a wall, that of the Gelotiana house on the Palatine in Rome. It mocks Alexamenos, a man who had the absurd idea of converting to Christianity. The clumsy engraver roughly reproduced the squashed features and blank gaze of the new Christian worshiping a crucified man with the head of an ass. If we can have any doubts about the resemblance between the graffiti and the real Alexamenos, we can be sure that the prankster wanting to ridicule a certain Rufus was indeed inspired by the real face of his victim, with a seriously prominent nose.

So, voilà, the first function of caricature: to make fun of a particular individual, for the purpose of personal revenge when it is, as here, a private caricature. Or, in a semi-public form of mockery, to stigmatize an individual or a social or religious group like the new Christians here. But mocking a person using a picture was shrouded in a taboo that persisted until the end of the Middle Ages. Image is at the heart of a powerful division within religions when it comes to representing the divine. Theologians had protracted debates on the question. We will later see this dispute continuing even today with the painful history of the Muhammad caricatures in the 21st century. So, the subject is delicate. If individuals tried in those distant times to mock religions by means of images, it was on fragile materials that have miraculously survived.

Here we are on the border of what we call private humour and public humour. There is an immense distance between private comedy, which

# WHAT'S SO FUNNY?

takes place between four walls or specifically on the walls of houses, which is as old as the hills, and the public humour which is addressed to everybody. We can establish a middle category: semi-private humour, reserved for small audiences in the know who at least share a common value system. As long as societies were separated into strict social classes, where some have almost no rights and others highly-placed by birth or fortune have all the rights, the kind of humour circulating among common people was certainly private and anonymous. Thus, the perpetrators of these mockeries would incur no blame or punishment since they remained unknown. At the opposite pole, on the side of nobles and kings, it is hard to imagine a chief, king or emperor, worthy representatives of the divinity, offering an artist resources to engrave the noble's deformed features in stone to make people laugh!

## The Medieval Comic

Throughout the medieval period, which lasted almost a thousand years, laughter was viewed in an ambiguous way. A legacy of ritualized seasonal festivals, the collective habit of letting off steam with libations, buffooneries, and role reversals, spread out following the Greek Dionysia. Saturnalia and bacchanalia among the Romans, the feasts of "fools" and those of "asses" in the Middle Ages, charivaris, and carnivals almost everywhere and on every calendar.

First of all, the links between religion, laughter and ribaldry are found significantly in the main comic currents of the Middle Ages. During the rise of Christianity, two contradictory movements around laughter are to be noted, representing the continual tensions between two currents of thought. On the one hand, the Fathers of the Church condemned laughter, linked according to them to the pagan world, to the body, to the devil (Sarrazin, 1998). The same perspective will stealthily spread until the present day among religious partisans of extreme tendencies. On the other hand, there is a popular trend urging the public to laugh at everything, and especially at those who prohibit laughter!

Around the 8th century, in private circles within the Church, we know of joke collections intended for monks (Legoff, 1989), the *roca monacorum*. Regarding semi-private humour, the lives of saints of that period were sprinkled with comic passages to attract new devotees. Likewise, sermons by popular preachers laughing at the faults of their contemporaries were preserved; copyists transmitted *exempla*, which consisted of short moralizing tales provoking laughter among the churchgoers, largely made up of women, more fervently religious than their husbands!

This second universe is one of court fabliaux, poems sung by troubadours intended for a restricted audience of nobles or bourgeois. Fabliaux can be very daring, openly mocking the depraved mores of prelates, describing in detail how priests have often been the lovers of married women, for example. In addition, mockery spreads in the churches, through the beggar preachers, who, enjoying a certain freedom around the 13th century, openly mock in the pulpit lustful and greedy monks and priests, portraying here again how these hypocrites engage in acts contrary to their teaching (Roy, 2011). It must be remembered that even if these songs were reserved for noble audiences, multiple ears also heard them: servants, bodyguards, various others in the service of the powerful. And they surely were happy to spread these songs widely.

The decadent clergy remained the target of derision in the farces, those medieval plays performed at fairs (Minois, 2000) undoubtedly inherited from Latin comedies. The stereotype of the sinful priest made a strong impression because religion was so important and if you think about it, this genre of laughter was above all moralizing rather than subversive.

We have seen that the Church vigorously condemned laughter as demonic; it lowers man to the rank of the beast, which in itself is very funny since beasts do not laugh, except probably monkeys, according to the latest research! But people wanted to laugh, they needed it like oxygen. So, they used subterfuges to disguise laughter. The gargoyles of the cathedrals had the same function as the horrible little gods of immemorial times, they chased away evil. With their rolled-back eyes, grimacing facial expressions and fantastic animal shapes, they heralded future caricatures. And then, in fairs, comic stories are told, funny situations are exposed by amusing puppets. With the rise of the bourgeoisie in the Middle Ages, comes the development of a new type of sung recitation, the fabliau. After being created in the noble courts, it spread among the people. As the Middle Ages advance, the fashion for fabliaux extended to all social classes. The fabliau, halfway between the courtly romance and the *lai* or short lyrical poem, often populated by animals, spirits and witches, ridicules the customs of its time (Roy, 2011). Then, it would be sung by the troubadours to an illiterate public with many funny subjects seasoned with saucy allusions and laughable disguises: fickle women, bawdy priests. What about coarse songs, drinking songs,

## WHAT'S SO FUNNY?

or even, obscene songs? They were disguised for pious or childish ears thanks to savory puns, and have come down to us through oral tradition. Finally, seasonal festivals of great fun such as fools' or donkeys' feasts, carnivals, hullabaloos were tolerated. Voilà for public art.

All other forms of laughter were private and semi-private. For instance, was the king's jester intended for everyone? No, on the contrary, his function was restricted to the court. His indispensable role appeared as far back as among the Greek and barbarian rulers (Minois, 2000) and this tradition continued until the classical period. Funny detail: queens also had their jesters! And then the fashion spread to all the nobility! The fool is ugly, sometimes misshapen, a dwarf or hunchback, and he says whatever he thinks. Sometimes, he is a real fool, but more often than not, he is very intelligent. Because you must be very clever to know what to say and not to say! The jester performs the role of the opposition or of revolt. The truth comes out of his mouth. But this truth remains encoded, discreet.

## The Renaissance

During the Renaissance, two currents of inspiration ceaselessly intertwined to give birth to comedy as we know it. On the one hand, a popular oral tradition was developed over the centuries in fairs, public markets, shows performed in castles (farces, fabliaux) or in churches (mysteries) by minstrels, traveling actors and clowns, who themselves were inspired by Greek and Latin traditions transmitted both orally and literarily. On the other hand, authors such as Shakespeare or Molière wrote plays and texts that have come down to us more or less intact. Many exchanges, borrowings and influences connect these two universes. What is fascinating is that these comic situations were used afterwards by silent cinema, then by comic cinema, finally by comic strips and cartoons, in a joyful saraband where human stereotypes and eternal misunderstandings have been endlessly transposed.

Of course, there were also literary writings. Strangely, a truly anticlerical work of literature appears via the pen of a monk. Shameless salacity, sacrilegious remarks, everything was over the top in the work of François Rabelais (1483–1553), which sheds astonishing light on the intensity of laughter that shook Renaissance society. His works were condemned one after another by the Sorbonne. He calls his learned detractors therein "sorbonagres", a portmanteau pun comprising the institution's name and "onagre", the word for a wild ass. Rabelais, who began by signing the anagram of his name, Alcofribas Nasier, as camouflage, gradually received the protection of French nobles including François the 1st. Humanist genius, he earned his living as a medical doctor, while writing satires of his society, criticizing the abuses of the nobility and particularly those of the clergy and other religious people, accusing them of "papolatry" (*Fourth Book*). His work came in five major opuses: *Pantagruel* (1532–42), *Gargantua* (1534), *Third Book* (1546), *Fourth Book* (1548), *Fifth Book* (1564, posthumous); we will see an extract of his incredible pen in Chapter 8. He established a comic genre halfway between scholarly discourse and popular culture through his rude remarks and his immoderate taste for the excesses of good flesh and drunkenness – indeed, in the 1663 edition, Rabelais' work is termed "*Histoire satirique de son temps*" (Satiric History of his Time).

In the world of theater, commedia dell'arte is a genre developed in 16th-century Italy and characterized by improvised plays based on simple outlines and interpreted with masks and costumes. Let us reiterate that the tradition excluding women on stage continued, following the pattern of Greek and Latin comedies. Here again, masks allowed men to play all the female roles, as well as serving to establish a precise character's personality for the audience. The commedia dell'arte spread throughout Europe thanks to ambulant troupes.

IV. The "Doctor", from commedia dell'arte. All rights reserved.

# WHAT'S SO FUNNY?

Inspired as much by the Roman canvas of Plautus and Terence as by commedia dell'arte, Shakespeare (1564–1616) called his comedies romances such as *Much Ado about Nothing* (1600) - starring two couples, one romantic and the other, ridiculous — or *The Taming of the Shrew* (1623), which we will see in Chapter 5. Later, the comedies of Molière (1622–1673) include magnificent works like *The Miser* (1668) where a cartoonish miser wants to marry off his reluctant daughter, *The Imaginary Invalid* (1673), a scathing satire of the doctors of the time of which we will see an extract later, and *The Amphitryon* (1668) deploying irony in successive illusions through multiple disguises. These wonderful comedies, which have survived through centuries without a wrinkle, inaugurate the parade of great universal comedies. It should be noted these playwrights benefited from protection in very high places, without which they could not have taken such conspicuous liberties.

Medieval pranks, nursery rhymes and then the commedia dell'arte developed a whole anthology of grotesque personalities and ridiculous couples, several in constant opposition, the whole arranged on basic narrative diagrams. More or less at the same time, engravers, then designers extended their range by targeting the ugliest and therefore the funniest faces thanks to systematic deformation of each facial feature.

These findings, both thematic and formal, will constitute the basis of all the visual comic language of the following centuries. Let us go to Renaissance Italy to meet the first artists who systematically distorted features, hence the Italian expression "caricaturas" used by the English. They rediscovered the famous "ugly" opposed to the "beautiful" dear to Aristotle. Early Renaissance artists wielded some form of macabre and almost surreal visual discourse. The Dutchman Hieronymus Bosch (circa 1450–1516) painted fantastic, hallucinated creatures, with tortured and deformed faces, in works evoking hell, "The Garden of Earthly Delights, Ship of Fools". But the outbursts of mysticism that underlie his paintings prevent us from associating him with any kind of humour. Let us keep in mind he initiated a movement of systematic deformation of faces and bodies which will be imitated by many artists, including Breughel the Elder.

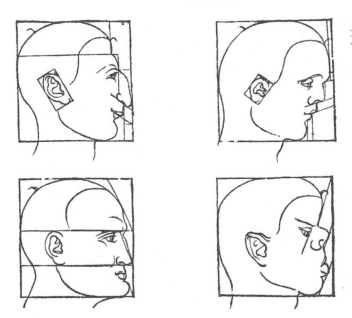

V. Dürer, *Treatise on the Proportions of the Human Body* (1523), woodcuts from drawings kept in Dresden.

The great German engraver and mathematician Albrecht Dürer (1471-1528) was already deconstructing the parameters of the human face in 1523 in a scholarly essay on the geometry of human bodies. In this sheet, as much as the two faces on the left can still be imagined, the two on the right are ridiculous. The engraver has so accentuated the angles of the facial features that he gives them a clownish look. Dürer enjoyed measuring the tiny degrees between normality and excess that others call comical.

Then, in Italy, engravers and artists, with Leonardo da Vinci (1452–1519) at the forefront, began to systematically dismantle the canons of beauty. The heads they designed are defined as being "loaded" or "carichi". Among others, Leonardo influenced the Carracci brothers around 1600, then Bernini.

# WHAT'S SO FUNNY?

VI. Gian Lorenzo Bernini, *Two priests with glasses*, circa 1650.

The approach of Bernini (1598-1680) was more oriented towards the distortion of a particular person's features. Having come to France to participate in the Louvre's reconstruction, Bernini entertained the Louis XIV court by drawing quick and funny sketches. We easily understand these drawings were exchanged inside a small circle and shame on whoever disseminated them among the people.

This is what we call private humour. This fashion for jokes in pictures spread across Germany and England, in royal courts and noble salons, which explains the availability of so many manuals describing the procedure of transforming jokes into images. The art of caricature became an upper-class hobby in 18th-century England. The first woman to invite herself into the cartooning circle deserves to be mentioned. The first booklet on how to distort line appeared in London, in 1757; the authors, Mary and Mat Darly, published a second one in 1762, with an interminable title: *A book of caricaturas in sixty copper plates with the principles of designing in that Droll and pleasant manner by M. Darly, with sundry Modern and Ancient examples and several well-known Caricaturas taken from the Tabernacles, Newmarket, Playhouses, etc. etc. To be held of Mary Darly in Ryders Court near Cranbourn alley, Leicester Fields*. Mary engraved all of the drawings and wrote a few texts, which is very interesting to know, but unfortunately no illustrations remain from these two booklets. The earliest known caricatures in Canada belong to this category of small drawings for private circulation.

VII. George Townsend, *"More Disgraceful Laxity"*, 1759.

Text of the balloons: "Evidement (sic), les espions puants sont ici! Plus de trahison! Et puis, une dame! (Obviously, the stinking spies are here! More betrayal! And then, a lady!) George Townsend, British Brigadier General, formerly Major General Wolfe's second, amused himself with his superior's obsession for the cleanliness of the battlefield latrines, on the Plains of Abraham, during the War of Conquest! We can laugh with him about the compulsive thoughts of his superior, but also about the triviality of Townsend if not about his questionable jokes. He reduces his chief to a poor scared person seeing spies everywhere, even in the closets.

A few years later, the Englishman Grose also authored a manual explaining the steps to follow to draw caricatures that in many ways evoke Dürer's engravings.

## WHAT'S SO FUNNY?

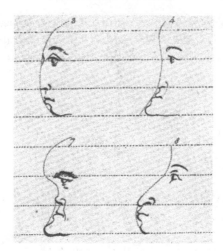

VIII. Francis Grose, *Rules for Drawing Caricaturas*, London, 1788.

> Grose (1731-1791), an Irish draughtsman and lexicographer, has the same manner as Dürer of distorting the features with a quasi-scientific approach. Geometric curves systematically deconstruct the architecture of the face, to the point of ridicule. If Dürer tried only to understand the human face and its representation, Grose had an avowed comic purpose. We can see that he was curious about all kinds of oddities: he wrote, among other things, a Dictionary of the Vulgar Tongue (1785)!

Initially a private leisure activity where nobles exchange mock portraits of each other, caricature gradually evolves to make fun of public figures through the nascent press. It criticizes their actions with the goal of getting them either to change or to step down. This stage, which remains current, was only reached with the advent of revolutions and the separation of Church and State. At this point, highly critical speech, previously the strong point of theatrical comedy, will gradually slip into satirical journals during the 19th century.

Before getting to the heart of the matter, let's spend a moment on the concept of humour. The term "humour" first appears in England. The etymology of the word "humour" can be traced back to the Latin word *umor* referring to vital bodily fluids. The Englishman Robert Burton (1576–1640) is one of the first to use the word "humour" in English in *The Anatomy of Melancholy* (1621); he says that "black bile advances the conceptions of men more than any other mood and improves their meditations more than any strong drink or white wine" (Quoted by Pollock, 2001). The same word is used in English, French, Italian and Spanish. Someone evoking humour in those days first thought of bodily humours. Without wanting to make too long a story, let us say the mood that most attracted the attention of philosophers and then researchers was black bile or melancholy. The term "spleen" for a sad mood derives etymologically from *splen*, the organ secreting bile.

From the Greek Aristotle (*Problema XXX*) to the Greek Democritus (*On Laughter and Madness)*, the link was made between a melancholic feeling and laughter. Two mental states looking like opposites were associated by theorists. There is something disturbing in this shortcut between a gloomy state of mind and the often-sudden burst of laughter. One must believe that laughter is not as light as it seems and can instead come from intense sadness. It is well known that many comic writers, humorists, and cartoonists have been or are in fact very tortured and melancholic beings. Let us keep in mind this strange association: it will allow us to shed a special light on certain types of humour, including dark humour and nonsense.

Some philosophers also draw a parallel between laughter and madness, but a controlled madness, that of the jester. Whether it is Carlo Buffone and Malicente in Ben Jonson's (1572–1637) *Every Man in His Humor* (1598) or Feste and Malvolio in Shakespeare's *Twelfth Night* (1599), the shock of these two excessive human traits is to be noted as a beginning of the modern notion of humour.

But we won't try to define "humour", following the lead of researchers who talk about "the impossible definition of humour" (Attardo, 1994 and Escarpit, 1960). We will look at how its different processes have evolved.

Thus is the table set for the emergence of completely secular and democratic humour. If we want to succinctly summarize this entire evolutionary movement which we will see in detail in later chapters, let us say that the rise of parliamentarism spreading ideas of freedom across Western countries and, secondly, technological advances eventually bringing in the mainstream press, photography and soon cinema, both open the door to unconstrained humour within everyone's reach. Narrative outlines of comic theater, facies, and gestures from early caricatures, the human stereotypes developed by these two pioneering art expressions, combined to give birth to new humorous forms. In the 19th century and at the beginning of the 20th, such creations would either represent movement or would really be in movement, starting with stories in pictures, then comic strips, and later, cinema and cartoons.

# CHAPTER 2

# EXAGGERATION

**E**xaggeration as a stylistic process amplifies reality like a magnifying glass to show its absurdity.

In everyday life as well, we often exaggerate to make people laugh. For example: "To split one's side with laughter," "His Dumbo ears are flapping in the wind", "She could gnaw wood for a beaver dam with those buck teeth", "Her nose would turn an anteater green with envy", all are colorful expressions amplifying reality for fun. Indeed, anyone looking for a laugh will exaggerate a story to capture the audience's attention: depending on their gifts, storytellers may accentuate the voices of the characters involved, raise the female tones, deepen the male register, or make the speech nasal or lisping. One can also accelerate the rhythm, multiply the hassles, or enlarge the problems. Amplification is a variant of exaggeration, increasing the intensity of imitation in facial features or in the objects of another artistic work such as pastiche or parody.

Amplification of facial features or body proportions for a satirical purpose is probably as old as the hills. Instantly perceptible, amplification also takes place on the metaphorical level, coming often from an unconscious association between physical and moral deformation. Among the oldest examples are the masks of Greek comic theater, which distort the mimicry produced by various characters. The Greek mask contained a megaphone for a mouthpiece to amplify the voice, thus serving a practical purpose. More importantly, the mask emphasized emotions and attitudes. In comedy, masks freeze grotesque grimaces for the actor. To modulate his

# MIRA FALARDEAU

theatrical performance, because nobody could see his face, the actor had to amplify not only his tone of voice in line with the emotions to be evoked, but also to accentuate his gestures to get the message across. The mask would multiply such artifices: the person behind the mask was first magnified by this subterfuge. He would become someone else. The comic mask transformed the actor who thereby would reach a second nature, according to theatrical conventions: he was playacting. After that, he climbed to yet another level, because of the role imprinted on this artificial face. The mask could transform the man into a woman, the slave into a god, the valet into a master. The frozen mimicry of puppets and the red nose of clowns derive from these comic codes.

The mask, tragic or ritual, basically retains its comic side when shifted from the stage to the street to become an essential element of a carnival. Moreover, the festive mask allows any man or woman in the street to play a role, what an exquisite pleasure, and to pull out all the stops since no one can recognize them. Indeed, the etymology of the word "person" is associated with the word "mask" — *persona* in Latin, "actor's mask" — which portrays a character.

In popular festivals, everything is excess. So, from their inception, we see in comic spectacles what Bakhtin (1968) calls the carnivalesque, an exaggeration of various comic processes to the point of paroxysm. The origin of "carnival" lies in the "naval chariot" or boat on which the god Dionysus was perched and taken out on the streets during festivities. A carnival releases pent-up steam, for which laughter is the safety valve. Despite the fact we are here in a grey zone where the sacred and the profane overlap, we cannot deny the link between laughter and exaggeration: they are intimately linked.

We must not turn away from exuberant laughter under the pretext that it breaks out in religious settings. In those ancient times, was it possible not to be religious? Don't these exaggerations precisely show that nothing could prevent the populace from giving themselves over to moments of tomfoolery? Then cults and, later, churches had no choice but to integrate such fun into their rites. Sarrazin (1998) says that the preacher's paradoxical fusion of fear and laughter creates an ambivalent "joyful fear". Through this antithetical concept of "joyful fear", he associates comedy with the fear of breaking all barriers. Indeed, the crowd's laughter is linked to a kind of intoxication, real or imagined, that could lead to scoffing at prohibitions, overthrowing taboos. Consequently, this laughter would finally be freed from ecclesiastical constraints in fairground theaters, with extravagant gestures during painless battles and with harmless blows from dummy clubs. For more than a millennium, popular art held the keys to outrageous laughter.

I. Leonardo da Vinci, "*Grotesque Heads*", ink, circa 1530.

The great artist and inventor Leonardo da Vinci (1452-1519), after having penetrated the essence of human beauty, scrutinizes the abysses of ugliness. Leonardo adds volume through the shading, so its accentuated wrinkles and folds seem more pathetic on that poor old woman and more laughable to us! To study its principles, the artist lengthens and systematically stretches the physiognomies. What enjoyment to contemplate these faces thus distorted!

The Renaissance brings in turn a renewal of the art of laughter, especially from the pen of great masters. Excessive accentuation of facial features becomes droll, as we have observed. Studies systematically distorting faces emphatically become the starting point for a new art: caricature, even though, at first, artists claim their drawings are mere exercises in style. Indeed, the faces do not represent known persons. They just stand for Mr. and Madam Everyone. Clearly, there is no criticism behind them; just exaggeration of lines, forms and expressions for pleasure's sake, as we can see in Hogarth's study.

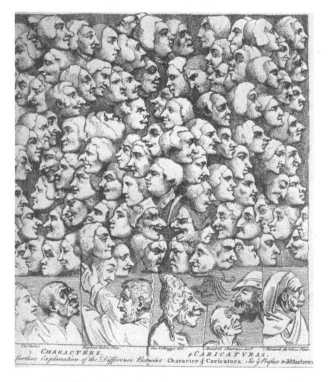

II. William Hogarth, "*Characters and Caricatures*",
engraving, middle of 18th century.

In the 18th century in England, William Hogarth (1697-1764), painter and engraver, and his associates, refined the expression of faces and silhouettes. Hogarth saw himself as a moralistic painter, choosing to denounce the decadence of his time by illustrating the excesses of his contemporaries. Here, Hogarth probes the line between a realistic face and its caricature. In other words, he tests the boundary between reality and exaggeration. He seems to play the game of retaining the form within the limits where the charge does not yet appear, then suddenly, unleashing his pen until the faces are deformed. The frame of the engraving wherefrom faces seem to emerge accentuates the volume of the deformations. The circus of sneering facies piled on top of each other radiates an atmosphere at once grating and dehumanized. In fact, this accumulation adds to the sensation of drollery, as in a crazy crowd.

Following Hogarth, another English artist, Thomas Rowlandson (1756–1827), painter and caricaturist, emphasized the eccentricity of behaviors and situations through irony. Another step forward was

## WHAT'S SO FUNNY?

thereby achieved; now artists could not only accentuate forms and mimics, but they could also criticize behavior. Inflating the bellies, puffing up the faces, Rowlandson is one of the first to tell a story using etchings and to create a character, *Doctor Syntax* (1812–1820), whose misadventures delighted the passers-by gazing at the grotesque scenes in the engravings posted on the walls.

With the Spaniard Francisco de Goya (1746–1828), painter and engraver, grotesque speech became morbid. For his part, Baudelaire, (1821–1867), the French poet, ingenious translator of Edgar Allan Poe (1845), referred to: "[...] the very rare element Goya introduced into comedy: I mean the fantastic. Without doubt, he often plunges into fierce comedy and rises to absolute comedy". Here we face a confusing amalgam of humour and melancholy, called *"humeur"* in French, which recalls the common source of the two concepts. Humour is not just what creates laughter; it can also be what produces reflection.

With the advent of parliamentarism and the birth of modern democracies, newspapers developed and, after them, satirical newspapers grew throughout the 19th century. Another word for portrait caricatures, the *portraits-charge*, wherein one highlights the features or the defects of a person by enlarging the face, as the name indicates, became more and more fashionable. Often though, their creators had to undergo the wrath of Justice, as the comical episode of the pear of Louis-Philippe, from Philipon, humorously demonstrates (see Chapter 8 on anthropomorphism). Mordant and ironic texts are peopled with caricatures and stories in images — ancestors of comics - wherein the great of this world and contemporary mores are mocked. Chronicles are full of puns, riddles, word games, and authors put their hearts into the charges against the leaders. This mixture of caricatures, comic texts and corrosive chronicles became a winning recipe for the multitude of satirical newspapers swarming throughout the 19th and a good part of the 20th centuries, in all Western countries. Some newspapers became known all over the world such as one of the first, *Punch* (1841–1992, 1996–2002) of London. Let us insist: democracy and parliamentarism were born at the same time as caricature, which is no accident. With the corollary that dictatorships hate corrosive humour and caricature in particular, as we will see later. Following the emergence of major newspaper chains in the 20th century, caricature found a place therein , but remained very critical in the satirical magazines which were becoming more and more mordant.

## MIRA FALARDEAU

The industrial revolution and its myriad innovations coupled with rising standards of living and the emergence of a new middle class eager for leisure led to new and often interrelated inventions following one another at full speed. The accelerated pace of *commedia dell'arte* narratives, where misunderstandings and turn-arounds come together at a rapid pace, had already entertained generations and generations of audiences of all ages and classes frequenting fairs and festivities. Now came Boulevard Theater, burlesque cinema and cartoons reproducing these jerky movements. Photography brought new keys to understanding the mysteries of movement and helped stories in images to break out of their immobility. Thus, comic strips appeared as an art of fast narration and of special effects movement. At the turn of the 20th century, comic strips, comic cinema and animated cinema arrived at the same time. All of them generated the same kind of fun with breathtaking situations in ultra-fast movements presented or evoked. The vibrations of movement were further accentuated by jumps of images due to technical deficiencies in the newborn cinematograph. Unbridled chase scenes and repetitive kicks were linked at full speed in the burlesque cinema, carrying the art of slapstick, a series of blows with a stick, to its peak. Cartoon art then took over with endless chases between dogs and cats, cats and mice and *tutti quanti*. Comic strips configured emphasis with onomatopoeias and movement lines. People of all ages thrilled to the frenzied velocity of the action scenes and laughed instantly.

Comic cinema shone with its stars' grimaces and incessant trepidation. From the antics of the great Charlie Chaplin (1889–1977) and Buster Keaton (1885–1966), comedians' irresistible tics became highly recognizable and spread so much that these famous figures became symbols of comedy films. Jerry Lewis, Louis de Funès, and closer to us, Jim Carrey, Robin Williams or Jean Dujardin: the mere mention of their names steers laughter. Stammering, ragged eyes, explosive fury, eccentric jumps, everything in their performances seems straight out of a sudden neurological disease hitting them by mistake. And we laugh unreservedly! Regarding ultra-fast action, a movie series like *Home Alone* (dir. Chris Columbus, USA, 1990) and *Home Alone 2* (1992) looks like a masterpiece of the genre, particularly for the sequences where the two hapless burglars with frightful smiles and borborygmus from beyond the grave, attack the cute little blond boy (played by Macaulay Culkin), without suspecting that he will not

## WHAT'S SO FUNNY?

only give them a taste but dose after dose of their own medicine. The film *101 Dalmatians* (dir. Stephen Herek, 1996), written by the same scenarist, John Hughes, plays on the same hysterical mood, but we don't laugh with as much gusto as in *Home Alone*, whose recipe cannot easily be duplicated. TV series and Web series, in turn, use the same proven recipes.

In cartoon films, the link between speed and laughter is extremely tight because of the fantastic situations: *Woody Woodpecker* (Walter Lantz, 1940–1972), for example, unreels in the register of pure exaggerated movement. If we jump to the current era, almost every animation feature is conceived in such a rapid rhythm, often inspired by video games like *Angry Birds 2* (Clay Kaytis and Fergal Reilly, 2019), that one has difficulty breathing between successive ultrafast scenes.

Black humour, when humour marries the morbid, generates a language of excess, especially prized by the artistic and literary movement called surrealism in the early 20th century. Such humour, spreading through restricted circles, experimental journals and in avant-garde theater, flirts with the absurd. In general, the art of excess coupled with the grotesque and the outrageous developed mostly in closed circles of initiates throughout the 20th century. As long as these art forms did not reach beyond the cenacles, they were tolerated. When artists wanted to broadcast them for the general public, problems with censorship began.

The case of "horror comics" is interesting because of the influence they exerted. During the 1940s, American artists tried to free themselves from the atrocious images they had seen during the war by drawing them for more or less ironic comics, with a rather grating sense of humour. Very strict laws quickly interrupted their catharsis, but by the mid-1960s, they reappeared as a genre in their own right, and also in manga (Japanese comics). Then, began a kind of cat and mouse chase between legislation and humour of excess.

The counterculture resulting from the student protest movement and more broadly from the cultural revolution of the 1960s, spreading through Western countries, contributed to considerably stretching the boundaries of excess in the arts in general. In comics, texts and images alike were affected by this trend; visions provoked by drugs associated with the liberalization of morals and generalized protest against the "conventional" way of life almost exploded the codes. The most extreme movements were born in the underground press,

# MIRA FALARDEAU

in fanzines or fan magazines called comix, which by definition break the rules.

Then, on account of this growing success, the authorities slackened their vigilance and everybody could enjoy magazines like *Help* on which the American cartoonist Crumb collaborated, in 1965, with his emphatic lines and narrations which will become the signature of underground comics. Chronicles, comic drawings and comic strips came together in a new press always toying with the limits of acceptability.

This practice was accentuated in Europe with iconoclastic magazines such as *Hara-Kiri, journal bête et méchant* ("*Stupid and Wicked Review*") (1960–1985), which gave birth to *Charlie Hebdo* magazine in 1970. Following the American counterculture press, *Hara-Kiri* and then *Charlie Hebdo* were aimed at a select audience already converted to their viewpoint. Unfortunately, things definitely changed with the advent of Internet and its wide distribution. Over several decades, the always irreverent *Charlie Hebdo*, where everything was said and shown, had become accustomed to laughing liberally at all religions, especially Christian, Jewish and Muslim. Of course, religious satire was not its sole transgression, but only one among many others. The big difference, however, from anticlerical satires of past centuries, was that for the first time, it was attacking not only the majority religion, but also that of minorities, including that of new citizens with an immigrant background. *Charlie Hebdo* dared to show clerics adopting obscene postures or making scandalous remarks, so as to demonstrate the universality of human faults. Then, the advent of the Web advent confused the issue by opening up to a large and diverse audience this free and deeply skeptical discourse, still intended, as initially, for Western readers accustomed to such excess. The stronger the transgression, the more intense was the reaction. Outraged, religious extremists tried to silence the magazine through legal channels, then threats, finally going as far as terrorist actions, as we will see in Chapter 11. Despite trials and multiple bans, *Charlie Hebdo* continued on its path, making a prominent place for itself as one of the stalwarts of freedom of the press.

Moreover, as one of the founders of *Hara-Kiri*, Cavanna, says in his book *Bête et méchant* (1981): "Humor cannot be trivial. Humor is fierce, always. Humor strips naked. Humor judges, criticizes, condemns and kills. Humor knows no pity; nor half measures".

## WHAT'S SO FUNNY?

As we can see, the underground movement is still spreading in all the arts. In the underground press, scatology, pornography, hallucinations are commingled, in a loud scream against consumer culture.

III. Henriette Valium (pseud. Patrick Henley),
*Thousand rectums, it's a Valium album*, 1987.

**Henriette Valium (1959-2021) published in the USA and Canada as well as in Europe. The polyvalent Quebec artist, an illustrator as well as a musician, turns out to be one of the most outstanding representatives of the underground. Valium began in comics with the magazine *Iceberg* (1983 and 1986), ironically published in reaction to *Titanic* (1983-1984), and many far-out fanzines. However, he pursued a multi-faceted career: he added music, screen printing, collages, illustration, photo and video montages to his rich palette, bridging the gap between comics and the avant-garde arts. His boxes are dripping, half-human, half-molecular beings connected by pipes evoking the intestinal or genital world. His whole universe pulsates and erupts in a deeply critical discourse. The proliferation of lines creates a feeling of suffocation, Valium metaphorizing the human choking in the contemporary world.**

Women were largely absent from the field of humour before the middle of the 20th century. However, they took their revenge in underground cartooning, which was more easily accessible to them than the mainstream branch of comics and caricature, traditionally occupied by male artists.

IV. Trina Robbins, *Trina's Women*, 1976.

The American Trina Robbins (1938- 2024) was the trailblazer of this movement with her *It Ain't Me, Babe* (1970), the first comix publishing only women. She was also a scenarist for some of the *Wonder Woman* cartoons. Terre Richards and Lee Marrs joined forces with Robbins in 1972; they started *Wimmen's Comix*, which continued to operate until 1992. They wanted to deploy a different discourse from that of the men producing pornographic art in their comix, asserting these phantasms did not correspond to women's. These forms of art, under the direction of women such as Robbins, were very imaginative and opened for a generation of women artists the doors of new subjects, denouncing gender inequality, violence against women, and putting forth lesbianism, free unions and free sexuality. The lot served with a language of excess.

## WHAT'S SO FUNNY?

Surfing this wave, Aline Kominsky-Crumb (1948- ) is surely one of the most original underground artists of that period. Her ultrapornographic art was astonishing; she contributed to many comics and also created solo works like *The Bunch's Power Pak Comics* (1979–1981) and *Love That Bunch* (1990). She also collaborated with her husband, one of the fathers of American underground comics, Robert Crumb, in *Dirty Laundry Comix* (1977–1977) and was the editor of *Weirdo* (1986–1993), well-known outlandish comix whose reputation went beyond the U.S. borders.

American women's comix of the 70s and 80s undoubtedly unfurled the most daring humour women artists have produced. Their influence has been felt all over the world.

V. Julie Doucet, "What an intense city", *Dirty Plotte*, self-publishing and Drawn & Quarterly, 1988, 2019.

The Canadian Julie Doucet (1965- ) has published in Robbins' *Wimmen's Comix* and also in *Weirdo*. *Dirty Plotte*, whose crude title is a mix of English and Quebec French joual, is a self-published comix from the beginning of her career, republished under the title of *Fantastic Plotte* in 2014 (L'Oie de Cravan) and in 2021 under the title of *Maxiplotte*, 2022, L'Association. In her early days, she worked most of the time with a white line on a black background, thereby highlighting the unreality of her staging as well as its tragicomic appearance. Here, "Julie" meets the city of the Big Apple and the flotsam and jetsam of the street is animated with movements and dialogue with her as if on a bad drug trip. The dark atmosphere and a proliferation of lines reinforce the harshness of her critical discourse against big cities. Author of about fifteen albums in English and French, Doucet is particularly fond of unabashedly pornographic scenes. She brilliantly shines through in tortuous tones where the strongly marked decor permeates the huts as if they were alive. With *Maxiplotte*, she won in 2022 the Grand Prize at The International Festival of Comics in Angouleme (France), being the fourth woman in 50 years to win this prize.

At the dawn of the 21st century, emphasis had become the norm of a new type of humour. Whether in stand-up, comic strips, manga magazines or on multiple comic websites and "memes", the crudest sexual allusions, the outrageously violent remarks, the self-mockery involving handicaps or racism scandalize baby-boomers while generations X and Y shriek with laughter. The new media sometimes spread images or texts of such virulence they seem a return to outlets of emotion animating the crowds running amok in the Middle Ages. As if obscenity, blasphemy, and cruelty formed an ambiguous dance between laughter and the grinding of teeth. As if laughter provoked by excesses was frightening but a relief at the same time.

# CHAPTER 3

# SIMPLIFICATION

**The simplification process removes all incidental elements of a form, a text or a situation to keep only what is essential.**

Specifically, comic simplification provides a unique feeling of underlying but essential intensity. Simplifying for the sake of simplicity has no funny function. What could be more boring than the icons indicating restrooms in an airport or requesting silence in a library? Such schematism is accompanied by no intensity, only a message.

Technically, it was drawing, and more precisely sketching, that generated the process of comic simplification. This most probably started with a sketch of a shape, first the face, then the silhouette hastily drawn on a wall or pottery. We saw in Chapter 1 the figures of our first two found graffiti, Rufus and Alexamenos; considering their traits, it is highly probable that their authors were amateurs! Later, simplification developed into a technique.

# MIRA FALARDEAU

I. Annibale Carracci, *Rittrati Carichi*, circa 1600

Eminent Renaissance painters, brothers Annibale (1560-1609) and Agostino Carracci (1557-1602), artists of the Palazzo Farnese in Rome, found relaxation and fun sketching in the streets the most comical human types. Faces and silhouettes encountered in everyday life took shape in their sketchbooks. Intuitively, they discovered funny forms, capturing mimicry and laughable figures. This was a revelation for the artists of that time, and many began to draw like the Carracci.

Annibale Carracci's series of notebooks were published posthumously by Mosini in 1646, who described Carracci's comic drawings as "caricatura". This habit of distorting faces quickly became a fashionable game among artists; in fact, their interest at that point was to capture anybody's face, but no one's in particular.

II. Gian Lorenzo Bernini, *Cardinal Borghese*, 17th century

# WHAT'S SO FUNNY?

The Italian artist Bernini (1598-1680), called "the second Michelangelo", was an expert in simplification. A stroke, a line, a point, and there it is: a face emerges from the sketch. Contrary to what a neophyte might think, the art of comic sketching is often the result of a long process of refinement. The Baroque sculptor imported the concept to France when he spent time there in 1665, and, to our knowledge, he remains the first to have caricatured public figures, high-ranking ecclesiastics, among others.

*Chapitre Sixième*

III. Rodolphe Töpffer, *Le menton* (*The chin*),
*Essais de physiognomonie*, 1845.

Unlike the Carraccis and Bernini, who were professional artists, Rodolphe Töpffer (1799-1846), a young teacher from Geneva, practised simplified drawing until it became a kind of stenography, because an eye disease prevented him from pursuing a career as a painter like his father. He had fun drawing picture stories, or according to the expression of his time, "literature in prints". Nevertheless, his father aroused his interest in the arts, and introduced him to, among other things, the caricatures of the English artist Hogarth. Beginning in 1827, Töpffer produced seven picture stories: in *L'Histoire de Monsieur Jabot* (Mister Jabot's Story) (1831-1833), a pretentious man mimes bourgeois manners as in Molière's *Bourgeois Gentilhomme*. In *L'Histoire de Monsieur Crépin* (The Story of Mr. Crépin) (1827-1837), he uses irony to attack insipid pedagogy, an environment the author knew well since he himself was a teacher. *Les Amours de Monsieur Vieux Bois* (Mister Old Wood's Loves) (1827-1837) makes fun of senile infatuations, while *Monsieur Pencil* (1840), targets the greats of this world, mainly politicians, scientists and artists. Progressively, he evolved towards ironic political criticism, which he forthrightly accomplished in *L'Histoire d'Albert* (The Story of Albert) (1845), an open satire against a contemporary politician that everyone could recognize: James Fazy, founder of the Radical Party. What is interesting in Töpffer's approach is his accidental discovery of an exploratory method to simplify facial expressions. He ended up passionate about the subject and published a treatise entitled *Essais de physiognomonie* (Physiognomonic Essays) (1845) in which he outlined his method. A face drawn at random, as simply as possible, has a precise expression. He developed small elementary profiles and, systematically varying each element of the face, he built up a lexicon of physiognomies from which he drew whenever he needed to. In *The Chin*, the gradual recess of the chin from the upper lip leads to many ridiculous mimicries, while neither eyes nor shape of face are shown. Let us compare the approach of the Carraccis and that of Töpffer: the former search for immediately perceptible reality in order to grasp it, the latter goes in the opposite direction, without a starting point linked to reality. But the lines

Töpffer draws are not abstract, because he knows that any drawing of a face, however schematic it may be, reflects a certain mimicry from the moment it is recognizable by spectators or readers.

Indeed, reading a schematic drawing does not refer necessarily to reality but rather to an idea one has of the object, or the person represented. It is extremely interesting to consider that readers mentally recreate the referent image, that they have a role to play in the process of decoding the image. Thinking that part of the pleasure of interpreting simplified images derives from our own creation, represents only one step further we gladly take. In his analysis, he set out a number of observations that art historian Gombrich (1960) sums up as follows: "… he (Töpffer) believes that it is possible to constitute a pictorial language without reference to nature, without any practice of drawing after model. The linear drawing, he assures, represents a purely conventional symbolism. […] In addition, the artist who uses stylistic abbreviations in this way can always count on the viewer to fill in the missing elements." Schematization is the extreme point of simplification, which in some cases almost reaches abstraction.

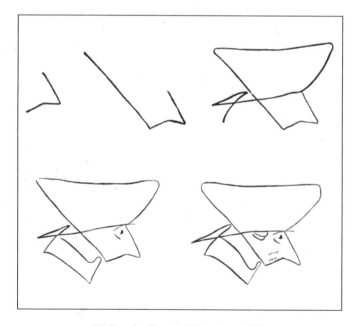

IV. Busch, *Der alte Fritz*, circa 1870.

## WHAT'S SO FUNNY?

The German artist Wilhem Busch (1832-1908) was certainly the spiritual son of Töpffer, first, because he was inspired by his system of experimentation on graphic abbreviation; second, because they were both creators of picture stories, the ancestors of comics. Busch has fun revealing the birth of the form just as in some cartoons a figure is being drawn as we watch. It is a game for Busch to extract Frederick the Great from a simple doodle, ridiculing him twice. On the formal side, he draws a silly and weak profile, and on the metaphorical one, he brings the great Frederick down from his pedestal, reducing his face to a little scribble. In 1927, *Koko the Clown* cartoons of the American Fleischer brothers continued on the road of slow transformations of form.

Later, Busch's famous picture story *Max und Moritz* (1865) will inspire Rudolph Dirks with his *Katzenjammer Kids* (1897) in *The American Humorist (New York Journal)* considered by some as the first comic ever published regularly anywhere. In the early days of comic drawings' expansion in newspapers, some cartoonists enjoyed discovering minimalist features for every expression.

Humorous drawing derives from caricature, except the person represented is not well known, let alone famous, just Mister or Madam Anyone. Launched in 1925, the *New Yorker* magazine adopted that new style of graphic humour, sophisticated and often nonsensical, eventually establishing a new trend.

V. Saul Steinberg, *All in Line*, 1945. All rights reserved.

The artist who succeeded in condensing line to the utmost, Saul Steinberg (1914-1999) was a pioneer among 20th-century cartoonists and he began drawing for the American liberal magazine *The New Yorker* in 1942. Steinberg's profiles are easily recognizable: two points for the eyes, an angular nose and a straight line for the mouth. This profile schematizing has been adopted by generations of drawers. It does not represent anyone in particular, therefore everyone. He created an abstraction of the average individual walking through a space, with a neutral and stable physiognomy, without decor, as if he were in a void. To quote a famous philosopher, we can say that Steinberg plays with Being and Nothingness. Here, in one of his most famous works, the artist questions, he enquires. He draws a hand which draws a human being which draws a hand which draws a human being and so on. This evokes the vertigo of creation where the line gives birth to a figure, born out of nothing. Or rather, the creator's hand gives birth to the figure, thus the artist can believe himself almighty. With Steinberg, we touch on philosophic questions about the sense of life and art.

In 1945, a selection of *The New Yorker*'s cartoons was exhibited at the American Embassy in Paris and the trend of sleek drawing became known overseas. This style almost turned into the hallmark of absurd humour in drawing. The French school of great illustrators, whose drawings are intentionally sketchy, clearly belong to this lineage: Sempé, Copi, Chaval and Reiser. After the Second World War, this absurd discourse will sound like a sigh of relief amidst horror. Each one of them expresses himself with an economy of line, all of them with their own tones and their discourses more or less soft or percussive, sometimes set off by texts antipodal to any gentleness evoked by the drawings.

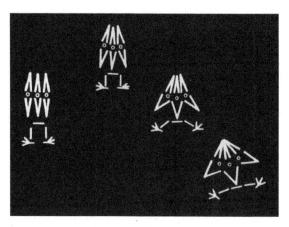

VI. Norman McLaren, *Blackbird*, ©NFB, 1958.

## WHAT'S SO FUNNY?

At the National Film Board of Canada, animation pioneers such as Norman McLaren (1914-1987) also played on the frontiers of schematization. McLaren, inventor of unique processes in animation such as scratching on film and pixilation, or frame-by-frame animation of people, adopted, early in his career, abstract animation with *Allegro* (1939), *Stars and Stripes* (1940), *Dots* (1940), *Loops* (1940). With *Blackbird*, he surpassed himself, illustrating the folk song "Mon merle ..." sung in French, with such economy of means the viewer comes out stunned by such magic. Circles for the eyes, V for the beak, lines for the legs, the codes twirl around in saraband to deconstruct and reconstruct a bird so pure in line that we end up seeing it as the quintessential bird.

VII. Pablo Picasso, "Guillaume Apollinaire", circa 1907.
All rights reserved.

The brilliant artist of Spanish origin but living in France most of his life Pablo Picasso (1881-1973), knew how to express in a few lines the bonhomie of the poet, his friend from the very beginning in the creative turmoil of Paris at the dawning of the 20th century. With that fat head rapidly dashed off, Picasso knew how to convey at the same time the simplicity of the poet and his intellectual weight.

# MIRA FALARDEAU

Et tandis que la guerre
Ensanglante la terre
Je hausse les odeurs
Près des couleurs-saveurs

Et je fu
m
e
du
ta
bac
de
Zo NE

(And while the war
Bloodies the earth
I increase the smells
Near the colors-flavors
And
I smoke
zoNE tobacco) ...

VIII. Guillaume Apollinaire, "Fumées" (Smokes),
*Caligrammes*, 1916, p. 71.

The French writer Guillaume Apollinaire (1880-1918) invented the word "surrealism" and also brought out the concept of "calligram", a visual poetry succulent and playful. In other words, as Apollinaire explained in a 1916 letter to André Billy: "Writing these poems where the typographical form represents the subject of the poem is an idealization of free-verse poetry". The poet jokingly associated the drama of war with the smoke he exhaled, shaping the ensemble into a pipe, as if performing a pirouette in the middle of the atrocities he saw and lived daily until he himself was wounded. The word "ZONE" is also an allusion to his seminal work "Zone". By his poetic game, Apollinaire here evokes the enjoyment of life stronger than pain, as if humanity would always win against stupidity and darkness. Apollinaire died in 1918, from a war injury inflicted in 1916.

# WHAT'S SO FUNNY?

William Shakespeare, *The Merry Wives of Windsor* (1660), Act V, scene V.

In theater and in performing arts, before the surrealists and the advent of the absurd, oversimplification was relatively rare. Nonetheless from time to time, we could notice minimalist dialogues as illustrated below in Shakespeare. In this conclusion of his comedy *The Merry Wives of Windsor*, Shakespeare describes in short and spare lines of dialogue the whole character of the larger-than-life Falstaff, decked out with faults, greedy for women, drink and culinary excesses, boastful and a liar but very clever. In just a few words, everything is said. Falstaff himself is rather flabbergasted by these barbs hitting so precisely as to leave him almost speechless.

FALSTAFF: "Seese and "putter"! Have I lived to stand at the taunt of one that makes fritters of English? This is enough to be the decay of lust and late walking through the realm.

MISTRESS PAGE: Why, Sir John, do you think, though we would have thrust virtue out of our hearts by the head and shoulders and have given ourselves without scruple to hell, that ever the devil could have made you, our delight?

FORD: What, a hodge pudding? A bag of flax?

MISTRESS PAGE: A puffed man?

PAGE: Old, cold, withered, and of intolerable entrails?

FORD: And one that is as slanderous as Satan?

PAGE: And as poor as Job?

FORD: And as wicked as his wife?

SIR HUGH EVANS: And given to fornications, and to taverns, and sack, and wine, and metheglins, and to drinkings, and swearings and starings, pribbles and prabbles?

FALSTAFF: Well, I am your theme. You have the start of me. I am dejected. I am not able to answer the Welsh flannel. Ignorance itself is a plummet o'er me. Use me as you will.

In comic texts, three figures outnumber the others in the inventory of economy of means: litotes (say less to mean more), implied (unsaid)

# MIRA FALARDEAU

and euphemism (say less to avoid shocking). Concerning euphemism, in real life, expressions are used to avoid shocking that can arouse laughter in spite of an ill-suited context. "He left us", (to go where? one would like to say) instead of "he died" seems particularly funny. In this vein of tragic alongside comic, it is common knowledge that one of the places where we laugh the most, discreetly, if necessary, is a funeral home. Litotes, unspoken words and euphemisms in terms and gestures, make this environment one of the most fruitful areas of comic condensation.

The theater of the absurd with its extreme simplicity became a genre in its own right during the 20th century. The playwrights Samuel Beckett (1906–1989) and Eugene Ionesco (1909–1994), respectively from Ireland and Romania, but living in France the greater part of their lives, crested that theatrical wave. Their plays are characterized by frozen dialogues, compressed gestures, action reduced to a minimum and comic intensity residing precisely in the apparent absence of feelings. They influenced many cinematographers, notably the great French director Jacques Tati (1907–1982) who excelled in this form of art. In his film *Mon oncle* (My uncle) (1958), among others, everything contributes to a comic effect caused by economy of discourse, gestures, facial expressions and action; even the soundtrack alternates everyday noises with actors breathing or whispering. The concept of absurd, which is the heart of Chapter 10, nonsense, has strongly influenced entire sections of contemporary culture through its democratization. It has become a new way of practising art, whether through pop music, video games or "Internet memes".

Simplification in writing leans towards degree zero. It flirts with trendy schematic design and minimalist abstract arts. Yet in humour, simplification maintains a balance, on a thin line, between restraint and silence, between whispering and saying nothing. Hence, by litotes or by irony, a soft whisper can harbor a restrained charge, suggesting: "see how my silence hides hustle and bustle"; or "I will say little because you already know what I mean"!

# CHAPTER 4
# SIMPLIFICATION/ EXAGGERATION

**G**o after the essence through simplification, then enlarge, amplify these features to make people laugh.

And voilà. But will the recipe succeed? As in gastronomy, you must master this art of reducing the sauce and then seasoning it vigorously! The table is set; it is now a question of enjoying subtleties. It is that mixed technique which Freud calls the process of condensation, talking about humour in his *Jokes and their Relation with the Unconscious* (1905): "Everything leads us to believe that the process of condensation drops certain elements subjected to it; the others then take charge of their investment energy, strengthen themselves through condensation or acquire an exaggerated force through it". The technique of humorous exaggeration/simplification could be compared to electrical oscillation, in varying degrees of intensity near one or the other pole, in a back-and-forth motion.

Using just one technique is not necessarily humorous. One can very well exaggerate without provoking laughter. Referring to caricatures, Bergson (1901) emphasizes that: "Without doubt, it is an art which exaggerates, and yet one defines it very badly if one designates exaggeration as its goal, because some caricatures are more lifelike than portraits, caricatures where exaggeration is barely noticeable, and conversely, one can exaggerate excessively without obtaining a real caricature effect."

On the other hand, as we have said before, we can just as easily simplify without being funny, which is what Michel Melot (1975) confirms: "[...] not all schematizations are funny, otherwise any sketch would make people laugh." It is from the friction of these two opposites that the spark of comedy will spring. He clearly indicates in which direction a schematization must go to become comic: "The first, and often the only one, of all the conditions required for a schematic drawing to become comic, is that its expressive force be schematized with it."

In such a way this art of caricature was finally able to flourish with the rise of democracies in the middle of the 19th century, coinciding with the arrival of satirical newspapers almost everywhere in the Western world. In fact, it is no coincidence that humour and democracy were growing hand in hand, feeding off each other.

I. Benjamin Franklin, "Join, or Die", *The Philadelphia Gazette*, 1754.

Published in Philadelphia in 1754 by the incredibly polyvalent Benjamin Franklin, as effective a politician and diplomat as a publisher and writer, the famous woodcut cartoon "Join or Die", considered the first editorial cartoon in America, speaks this language. The snake became the symbol of the disunion of the Thirteen Colonies during the French and Indian war and was shown later to drum up support for uniting in the struggle for independence. Two messages in one in the simplest way one can imagine.

The commedia dell'arte developed codes of condensed gestures that remain terribly effective to this day in transmitting the varied gestures

## WHAT'S SO FUNNY?

of pranks, vaudeville, clown and puppet scenes, even through motion machines, silent cinema, and later, cartoons and comics. The art of mime and clowning gestures conveys the basic vocabulary of comic movement. As we will reiterate throughout this study, condensing human movement by keeping only the essential passages is a technique used to show how social or political behaviours are often like a ballet or a ridiculous dance only intended to hide real intentions. Let us see the progress of the drawers during these years of discoveries.

II. Callot, "*Le joueur de violon* and *Le buveur vu de dos*"
(The Violin Player and The Drinker Seen from Behind), *Les Bossus*
(The Hunchbacks) series, etchings, circa 1621.

Fascinated by the commedia, the French engraver Jacques Callot (1592-1635) wanted to capture the multiple facets of a gesture in series such as *Les Caprices* or *Les Bossus* (1621). It is not by chance that these are series and not isolated drawings, Callot having felt the need, in order to properly describe the gestures, to illustrate them from different angles, a bit like a camera takes a circular travelling shot around its subject. In doing so, he not only looks for the appropriate attitudes but makes the viewer feel the dynamism of the scenes.

III. William Hogarth, *Gin Lane*, etching, 1750.

A fervent admirer of Callot, the English painter William Hogarth (1694-1764) staged real scenes in his engravings. A whole, teeming, grotesque little world is being portrayed in what he called his "silent theater": in order, he claimed, to correct the mores of his contemporaries, to paraphrase one of my favorite Latin proverbs "Castigat ridendo mores". He ridicules them by showing their excesses through human stereotypes that shift their zany silhouettes from vignette to vignette. There is the prostitution in *A Harlot's Progress* (1733) which he denounces or, in *Le-mariage-à-la mode* (1743), he laughs at the social conventions to which newlyweds belonging to the nascent bourgeoisie must conform, displayed like so many grimaces in a carefully orchestrated ballet. As he grew older, Hogarth employed a morbid or cynical language particularly relished by Anglo-Saxons, as in the plates of *Gin Lane* (1750) where the characters are competing to mime degradation by means of silhouettes bent over to the extreme, the one bowing under the yoke of age, the other weighed down by defects. The unfit mother drops her child, others gnaw the bones snatched from dogs. His series of engravings *The Bench* (1758) castigates the stupidity of professions held in high esteem by freezing the bumptious grandiloquence of haughty and hypocritical attitudes.

Daumier, the first great French cartoonist, took up the same theme in his series *Les gens de justice* (People of the Judicial System) (1847), and he felt the need to sketch more than one scene of declaiming lawyers so as to take a tour, in the literal sense, of their theatrical game and to ridicule its mechanisms.

Before the invention of photography, it is in engravings and drawings that one can find the essence of these comic gestures. In honing their skills at stereotyping comic gestures, artists showcased their discoveries, in the effort to outdo one another for the greatest pleasure of a public that was beginning, thanks to the parallel progress of printing and democracy, to enjoy the peace and quiet of what would be called freedom of the press and freedom of speech. Even though the history of these artists is riddled with ups and downs, censorship and imprisonment, followed by flashing rises to stardom.

In the preceding chapter, we saw Wilhem Busch as an incredibly talented innovator, playing with lines, summarizing in a mere handful of them a vigorous discourse, as in his "Der Alte Fritz". This precursor of comic strip art has created a true "pantomime in pictures".

IV. Wilhem Busch, *Max and Moritz*, 1865.

The two kids *Max and Moritz* (1865) by the German artist Wilhem Busch (1832-1908) rejoice in their mischief by hopping as if they were hanging from wires, dangling over the ground like marionettes, rather than leaning on it. Their poor victim seems to be walking in place on a conveyor belt, his torso forward to face a nonexistent wind, his knees sagging before he gets home to light his dangerous pipe. The explosion shows him falling flat on his back, an amplified posture typical of future comic-strip gestures. The work of this visionary is a chronicle full of vitality of 19th- century bourgeois Germany. He will strongly influence the author of the world's first comic strip, Dirks, in the creation of his *Katzenjammer Kids* (1897).

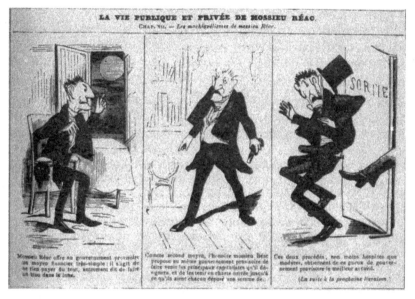

V. Nadar, *La vie publique et privée de Mossieu Réac*,
(The public and private life of Mr. Réac), 1848.

Nadar (pseudonym Gaspard-Félix Tournachon) (1820-1910) became one of the pioneers of photography. But, in his youth, he dabbled in caricature; he published in *Le Charivari*, then embarked on picture stories. The story of Mr. Réac was born amongst a group of Republicans who in 1848 opposed Prince Louis Napoleon. Hetzel, a member of the government, created *La revue comique à l'usage des gens sérieux*, (The Comic Review for the use of serious people) and sought out talent such as Balzac and Nadar. The latter depicts an opportunist, Mr. Réac, who is seen here contorted in various pantomimes. In Box 3, he seems animated by successive jolts that overlap in the same image, a classic special effect in the future art of comics. Condensation of several movements in one box, symbolizing a precise moment, creates the effect of rapidity if not simultaneity.

## WHAT'S SO FUNNY?

Very great authors, such as Balzac under a pseudonym, in *La Caricature* (1830), and very great artists, such as Picasso, as we have seen, have dabbled in humour. We cannot name them all because the list would be endless. It would be easier to name those writers or painters who have never toyed with humour!

At the beginning of the 20th century, comics are beginning to inundate not only the children's press but also the dailies, read by all, their easily decodable images having a formidable appeal for the often newly literate readership of the mainstream press. Comedy on stage is experiencing a decline in popularity due to more easily accessible movie theaters, showing both new film comedies and cartoons, again aimed at all audiences.

Editorial satire and caricature assumed the role of the court jester but extended to the wider public: they took on the role of a counterweight to the exercise of power. Following in the footsteps of the satirical press, it was the mainstream press that disseminated new ideas, including critical humour. To do this, it showcased cartoonists and columnists, who played their roles for an even wider audience: illiteracy was declining and reading the newspaper was becoming popular. As for reviews and magazines, their type of humour became more goal-oriented, more extreme, either more politically partisan or more ideological in nature. There have been Marxist, fascist, left-wing and right-wing satirical reviews.

In the first two decades of the 21st century, humorous websites have been taking over, rather like satirical newspapers, some of which have crossed borders while others have served local populations, some sites are better known than others, such as *The American Onion* (1988, website in 1996), a satirical site of comic false news. Comic radio stations on the Web also abound. Overflowing with creativity, this environment is ever-changing and the favorite sites of today may not be there tomorrow!

Since their inception, newspapers have supported the beginnings and development of the art of caricature. The current erosion of the daily press in favor of various information platforms seems to announce the fading of the art of caricature as the privileged language of freedom of expression. Only time will tell if this art is going to survive the current deep transformation of the mass media world.

# MIRA FALARDEAU

## Ideograms

One of the most original discoveries in cartoons and comics is the ideogram. Between word and image, this is the purest example of condensation, an image symbolizing an emotion or a sensation. The list would be endless: the black cloud for anger, the drops of sweat for effort or fear, the light bulb for a good idea! The ideogram can arise from a word game, like the expression "to see stars" illustrated by a myriad of stars, to mean dizziness or a knockout. Representation could also shift from one narrative plane to a more symbolic one, as when Pat Sullivan (1888–1933), the author of *Felix the Cat* (1926), has the cat's tail go from literal to typographic mode: the tail becomes a question mark! The lines of movement also conceal treasures of inventiveness.

Another subtle shift: the balloon, this device characteristic of comics which usually surrounds the words spoken, sometimes takes liberties. Now, is it not bursting from the thrust of the screams it contains, or maybe outlined in a zigzag to signify that the sound being emitted is from a radio or of thunderous volume? Or the balloon is empty: this indicates that its author is silent in amazement. Unless it contains big ones !!!! or some????

Ideograms are part of the vocabulary of world comics. In the world of manga (Japanese comics), which are widely distributed and exert considerable influence in contemporary cultural settings, the channels between comics, cartoons (*animes*) and films with actors are intimately linked. Inspired by ideograms existing in Western comics, manga have invented ideograms of their own and which can illustrate a host of emotions, sometimes quite zany ones. True poetry from comics and

## WHAT'S SO FUNNY?

*animes*, these little symbols constitute a second vocabulary outside the alphabet of letters. The manga have lifted the ideograms to such a level of sophistication that they deserve careful scrutiny.

The first great illustrator to use the term manga, Hokusai (1760–1849), celebrated for his famous *Great Wave in Kanawaga*, influenced 20$^{th}$-century European art, including Nabi and Art Nouveau. His work particularly affected pioneering American cartoonists such as Windsor McCay (1869–1934) in his *Little Nemo in Slumberland* (1905). Conversely, several great mangakas were inspired by Western comics, such as Osamu Tezuka (1928–1989), who claimed lineage from the Fleisher brothers and Walt Disney. As early as 1963, his *Astro* and his masterworks, such as *The Life of Buddha* (1972–1984), helped to build a flourishing language that made manga so strong that they had conquered the planet thirty years later. New arts have been born from this contact, including cosplay, theatrical games where everyone can participate, very popular among young teens; and video games, a great many of which present imaginaries from manga. It should be mentioned that western youth are currently very fond of reading manga and frequently use its codes in their own drawings.

The classic codes of the comic strip are known to all: the lines of movement follow the visual trajectory of an object or a person in the box, accompanied by beads of sweat which signify exertion while stars express pain, lightning, stupor or energy. Finally, concentric lines symbolize the extreme energy of which the pages of *Astro* provide eloquent examples. It's as if the atmosphere were turning into a solid and motion were etched into it as in clay.

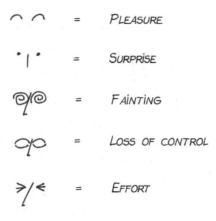

VI. Examples of current manga.

Manga has over the years added or reinforced its codes, which have now become essential to its language. The eyes, the basis of human expression, are particularly codified: round eyes surrounded by a circle imply a threat; the eyebrows in circles, pleasure; the eyes in dots, surprise; the eyes in a spiral, fainting. Some codes almost become language: white eyes mean loss of control; pinched eyes, effort; black eyes, emotion. The language of emotions is thus codified by symbols which become an alphabet for young readers.

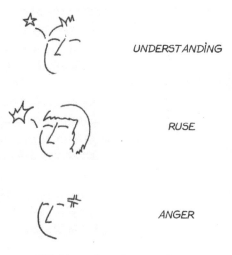

VII. Examples of manga faces.

The face is also codified: a face without eyes evokes an absence; a cross on the head expresses anger; a star in the eye, understanding; and lightning in the eye, cunning. The lower part of the face benefits from some easy-to-understand codes, such as shading for fatigue, shaded cheeks to signify discomfort, redness and fangs in an open mouth for rage; others are more nebulous such as the breath coming out of the mouth for disinterest. Finally, the mangakas dot the edges of the head with various very imaginative codes: flowers for happiness or gentleness, a spiral for naivety, circles for joy, concentric lines for attention. Condensation is found here in a form that is both refined and expressive.

In all types of comics and in all languages, onomatopoeias compete imaginatively to amaze the reader: perfect examples of the mix of simplification and exaggeration, the letters of the most diverse sounds and cries grow larger, retract, swerve in the fictional space of the bubble. A sequence of condensed gestures seasoned with ideograms and onomatopoeias is the site where the imagination of artists expresses itself. And the place where readers and spectators recreate this new world beyond reality, where everything is possible.

WHAT'S SO FUNNY?

AAAAH! GRRRʀʀ

## Stereotypes

For a character to become comedic, its author must synthesize, then magnify, an important trait. The same can be said of a theatrical character, just as in the movies or in comics.

In the commedia dell'arte, comedy is essentially a situation comedy, where various characters dupe each other in endless reversals of situation, called "misunderstandings" or "*quiproquos*" in French, from the Latin: "quid pro quo", literally to take one thing for another or one person for another.

Let us take a closer look at these stereotypes: in the beginning, there were four basic roles, two servants and two old men (Gebner, 2001). Among the valets, Harlequin is acrobatic, gluttonous, naive and Brighella, deceitful and venal; among the old are Pantalone, the father, a merchant and authority figure often outfoxed by young men madly in love with the beauties he marries thanks to his money, and Doctor, pedantic, sometimes a doctor and sometimes a lawyer. New faces followed: the talkative Punchinello and Captain Scaramouche. Later, others were added to this small comedy society whose pantomimes and puns delighted all ages. Indeed, the shows were intended for everyone because, surprising as it may seem, the concept of childhood only appeared shortly before the 19th century (Aries,1973). Assuming early maturity in children or childishness in the populace, these shows contained a little of everything. Yes, women's characters were missing! A female *zanna* (maid) finally appeared. But as long as men played women's roles, their acting scope was ambiguous and often full of innuendos on the world-upside-down theme. Anyway, to see men playing women's roles has always been comic for different reasons, including latent homosexuality or the presence of transgender people on stages, but also the fact that the public knew very well they were men. This led to double meanings including the reversal of roles!

VIII. "Pantalone", from commedia dell'arte. All rights reserved.

Whether in the comedies of Aristophanes or Plautus, or closer to us, those of Shakespeare or Molière, the same process of condensation is always at work. In Shakespeare's *The Taming of the Shrew* (circa 1599), the daunting Catharina makes us laugh with her mood swings and sharp repartee in an attempt to repel the amorous, and self-interested, assaults of crass Petruchio, who nevertheless wants to marry this rich thirty-something. In the next chapter, we shall look at the contrast within that original couple. Not only the characters but also the comic situations are standardized, both exaggerated and simplified to the maximum, thereby making them universal. In this way, comic patterns have been able to cross centuries and sometimes millennia without becoming dated.

Authors choose a typical character to concentrate on a flaw that they magnify to make the character ridiculous: the lazybones, the chatterbox, the parasite, the shrew. Faced with the stereotype, the public always recognizes someone. "Oh yes, so and so behaves like this, how ridiculous!" Both recognition and distance are being engineered in the process of condensation, and it is exactly this distance that creates the comic effect. The summit of the humorist's art is to make us believe he or she portrays other people, but not us! Oh no!

We are not moved by the sad adventures of the stereotypical, we laugh instead until we cry! The stereotype of the blunderer becomes an abstraction of all the blunderers in the world, and we can foresee

## WHAT'S SO FUNNY?

what will happen to him. Which, contrary to what you might think, is no less funny, but funnier.

The stereotypical couple is even more classic. The one and the other are no longer a pair but a being in itself. From the birth of com‑ics in daily newspapers, famous couples become the norm and from *Mutt and Jeff* (1907–1983, first by Bob Fisher) to *Jiggs and Maggie*, they amuse adults and children alike.

George Mc Manus, *Jiggs and Maggie, Bringing Up Father,* (1913- 2000)

> The "Art Nouveau" style of its first cartoonist McManus, all in curves and black zones, was instantly appreciated as much as were his themes. *Jiggs* and *Maggie* portrays an Irish immigrant couple in which the aspirations of the two spouses are different. While the gentleman, even if he became rich by winning the lottery, wants more than anything to remain as he always has been, a mason with his simple habits, like going for a drink or two with his friends at the neighborhood tavern, Madame absolutely wants to move up the social ladder, typifying the American dream. In fact, Maggie represents the modern woman, very elegant but also very self-willed. The two will clash with each other on this subject and many others, to the delight of readers, first American, and then from around the world, spreading out not only in comics but also in radio shows, in cartoons, in collections of comics, then in films. It is well known that reading comics in the daily newspapers of the early 20th century, so readily available, was a key factor in helping newcomers acculturate. Readers could often identify with this immigrant couple, contributing to the great success of this comic strip at home and abroad.

Indeed, throughout the 20th century, new media such as radio and television each in turn reproduced the patterns that had been transmitted to them. Radio comedy series often took over the funny characters known on stage or in the newspapers.

We can see that the arts of comedy are extremely porous, and heroes travel from comics to cartoons and from cartoons to movies with disconcerting ease. Thus, comic heroes are widely used in cartoons and then acted out in films, in different versions depending on

## MIRA FALARDEAU

the period. The same condensation processes are found in transpositions from one language to another, leading to just as much laughter even if we already know the end of the story! It is with the same burst of laughter that we can watch the same gags over and over again, and this movie or that comedy makes us howl with laugher, no matter how many times we watch it. *Airplane!* (1980, USA, dir. Abrahams and Zucker) is one of those gag anthologies, and a total mystery persists as to the real cause of laughter in the repetitive context of an umpteenth viewing.

Through their universality, *Tintin*, by Hergé (George Rémi, 1907–1983) with 23 albums (1929–1976), and *Astérix (1961- ),* by Uderzo and Goscinny with 35 comic books (1961- ), are also part of the heritage of works that span the centuries, human stereotypes rooted in the narrative patterns of Aristophanes and Plautus. Whether it is the transparent being that everyone can identify with, or the character of the runt who wins against the big bully, in the lineage of David and Goliath, these two mythical characters from the comics have crossed borders and have been translated into dozens of languages. Essentially, they represent, each in their own way, the success of the small against the great, of the weak against the powerful. And ultimately, of popular wisdom against the decisions of those in power.

Roughly speaking, we can say that there are two main classes of heroes: the atemporal heroes who span the world because their cause is universal, and the local heroes created by the local or an underground press because their subjects target a particular audience.

New funny stereotypes respond to old ones by adjusting to the flavor of the day. In reaction against the superheroes, comic antiheroes will multiply. As the name suggests, the antihero is the antithesis of the superhero: he is rife with flaws and faux pas. Like *Popeye, The Sailor Man* (Segar, 1929–1994), the public's favorite comic antiheroes evolve in a rather wacky world, exhibiting emphatic and colorful gestures, often to make fun of the superpowers of superheroes, which are quite repetitive and slightly boring. Popeye's famous gesture of tilting his head to slide the contents of a tin of spinach into his mouth, which gives him power, is a set piece. Again, there are the world-famous anti-heroes and the more local ones who more closely match the sensibilities of a

## WHAT'S SO FUNNY?

particular demographic. The antiheroes give readers or spectators a feeling of their own personal strength against all the rich and the powerful.

### Parody and Mediatization of Humour

Parody and pastiche regained their vigour with the surge of the mainstream press, radio and television throughout the 20th century. And what is parody, if not the act of choosing the most significant elements of the original work and exaggerating them to the point of ridicule? Later on, a second wave will invade social media, with a magnitude in exponential progression.

In fact, the craze for parody spread in radio comedy, then to television broadcasts, and now on Internet. One would make fun of this or that fashionable singer, this or that ad, or one or another television series. Monologists would frantically indulge in parody. Groups of humorists sprang up everywhere, performing first on radio, then on TV, and often in cabarets or in theaters, to boot.

A new genre of comics then emerged, the visual parody of the most popular entertainments, which would become almost a generic recipe for the entire world of comics for the remainder of the 20th century and the beginning of the 21st century. Magazines such as the American *National Lampoon* (1969–1998) set a precedent. They systematically distorted trendy movies or TV shows, as well as the covers of well-known magazines, and were understood only in their own cultural context. Each country obviously had its own parody magazine because jokes can only be fully understood by those who share the same culture. Parodic texts and photographs were accompanied by comics and derivative works that spread to radio shows, record albums, TV shows and movies. All this creative activity surged through the 1970s and 1980s, like a tidal wave.

Some concepts were gaining in popularity. One idea was to transpose the main dynamic of cartoons into television shows. The faces of politicians were transformed into grotesque marionettes in *Spitting Image* (Great Britain, 1984–1996). Then each country organized its own version of these satirical marionettes seasoned to the national taste. Their words were distorted to seem clownish, their mimicry and their jerky gestures evoked the circus, the fair. Here, the metaphoric sense is evident: the political world is like a circus.

## MIRA FALARDEAU

IX. Serge Chapleau, "*Et Dieu créa Laflaque* »
(And God created Laflaque), SRC, 2004–2019.

In these 3D animations, created by the editorial cartoonist Serge Chapleau (1945- ) of the Montreal daily *La Presse*, already well known for his love of "big faces", where he magnifies faces as if in distorted mirrors. The stereotypical character of the father, the principal character, is surrounded by his whole family, wife, son, daughter-in-law, father, even the dog; he is the maestro of this family saga complemented by scenes of pseudo information with zany comments on political and cultural news. The charged portraits of elected officials and well-known personalities are animated by elastic movements and jerky gestures generated by digital animation, giving a mechanical aspect to the whole, at the same time as a critical view of the profiles of the powerful.

Mixed parodic shows have abounded on TV, halfway between public affairs programming and comedy. Parody sketches follow one after the other, mocking social, artistic or political news. For example, *The Rick Mercer Report* (Canada, CBC, 2004–2018) and S*aturday Night Live* (NBC, 1975- ), whose team comes in part from that of *National Lampoon*, have special ties to politicians, and "invite" them to participate in their shows, and answer ridiculous questions or worse: they sometimes must perform foolish tasks. If politicians refuse to participate in such shows, they are so stigmatized that they end up giving in under pressure, either from the TV broadcaster or from their own press officer! As if the butt of the joke was now part of the process of mockery. "Let us laugh at me together instead of letting you laugh alone at me", the new breed of politician seems to be saying.

Another contemporary innovation: the animated cartoons that have popped up on some newspaper websites. For example, Ann

## WHAT'S SO FUNNY?

Telnaes (1960- ) publishes her animated cartoons on the *Washington Post* website. Her sharp, graphic style is driven by minimalist, jerky animation inspired by American UPA studios, known as "minimal motion animation". Sometimes, the scenes are constructed from real speeches or interviews with mocked politicians, which only adds to the zaniness. We see more and more newspaper websites experimenting with new formats.

In the 21st century, the new generation is definitely ensconced in virtual spaces, and social networks are becoming the new vectors of parody and pastiche. The parody genre which is all the rage today is undoubtedly the "meme". The "Internet meme" is flourishing on social networks like TikTok, Twitter, now "X" or Instagram, most often consisting of a photograph or video depicting a nondescript scene or familiar celebrities, of which a visual or sound (or written) element has been truncated, thus ridiculing the event or character in question. The peculiarity of the meme is its speed of transmission, which means that in a few minutes it can spread virally, ensuring instant popularity. Strongly influenced by advertising, it is also in the tradition of caricature through its critical bias. The public obviously needs to know the starting point of the meme to grasp its humour or the whistleblower intent.

But the danger of memes is that the broadcaster's goal is sometimes to lure the audience, then laugh at the "sucker punch", just delivered. The parody then has a dangerous tone that can go so far as to model itself on "fake news". It is then the creator's hearty laughter that is resonating and not that of the audience. In short, a whole new universe is taking shape through the instantaneousness of clicks, and the laughter is not always what you think: critical and acerbic. It can be complacent or complicit in half-truths, or downright fraudulent.

Memes serve as a barometer for freedom of expression, vying with each other in satirizing politicians. Countries with a dictatorial tendency do not really appreciate this tendency of young people to laugh at anything and everything, especially when official policies bear the brunt of the mockery. The meme's immediacy is also its strength, and it is hard to stifle in the age of super-fast social media communications.

But yet, this movement of unbridled laughter is being curbed in some countries. In fact, some regimes do go so far as to prohibit ironizing. To name just two superpowers, it is common knowledge that China has outright blocked Facebook and X sites. In compensation, it has started its own social networks such as WeChat and Weibo so as to keep a regular check on the content of the exchanges and to block anything it considers dissident. As for Russia, videos posted from abroad on the TikTok site – a social media controlled by China, whose comedy is one of the driving forces — have not appeared on Russian screens since March 2022, coinciding with the beginning of the war in Ukraine. Indeed, Russia has passed at breakneck speed a law condemning journalists and individuals who spread "false information about the government" to a maximum of 15 years in prison. The TikTok platform immediately reacted in Russia by blocking videos created outside of Russia.

We are curious to see how the Russian administration will react to the new dangers of emerging AI. You had to see Vladimir Putin's face, during his annual meeting with the public, in the second week of December 2023, when he was shown live in the presence of his own AI-generated clone, who asked him precisely: "How would you legislate about AI?" As the exchange was live, Putin became pale and flabbergasted, speechless… In AI, there is a territory of vast possibilities for fake news that we still have difficulty envisaging.

In short, we have been witnessing a crossover of bans and censorships in striking contrast to the great freedom of social networks in previous years. Consequently, this has crippled the possibilities of exchange for a whole range of humanity, mostly for a young audience. Farewell to a borderless globe of engaged and often humorous discourses allowing an easy outlet for so many people among various lands and cultures.

## Cancel Culture and Humour

In the West, where we are still dealing with democracies, for the moment, the more critical humour is at the forefront, the more we wonder if we can laugh at everything or just how far can laughter go. The question could not be more topical.

Let us see how a current of thought, initially respectful of diverse outlooks but which has swung into excess, is turning the world of laughter upside down. Cancel culture consists of denouncing and erasing by various methods the names or activities of people who in the past or in recent times have exhibited so-called reprehensible behavior or used derogatory words, as we will analyse further in Chapter 11. By extension, it comes to stigmatize any show or

# WHAT'S SO FUNNY?

artistic manifestation expressing or implying an ideology contrary to "political correctness", specifically irony towards racialized people, LGBTQ +, disabled persons, visible minorities, women. That movement has been raging for several years now, ravaging so much material that it is actually difficult to quantify. It has swept like a tsunami over our societies. Social networks have been the amplifier.

An excellent example is that of the "biter bit "in the case of Dave Chappelle (1973- ). In October 2021, this American stand-up comedian aroused the ire of LGBTQ + movements in his show on Netflix, "The Closer", where he was defending J.K. Rowling, the famous author of *Harry Potter*, accused of "transphobic" remarks. He took advantage of her standpoint to be ironic in the current debate on the notion of gender. This humorist, himself racialized, suddenly became the victim, to his own surprise, amidst an outburst from social networks and associations. In short, this illustrious defender of the rights of Blacks was accused of homo- and transphobia, when he was under the impression of defending those communities! This event shines the spotlight on the difficult coexistence between humorists and minorities, as well as on the spectre of self-censorship in the world of humour.

During this same month of October 2021, the Mike Ward vs Jérémy Gabriel Judgment rendered by the Supreme Court of Canada concluded years of legal battle around a Ward show. In his 2010–2013 shows, the Montreal humorist made fun of Jérémy Gabriel, a young disabled boy who had sung at the age of nine for Pope Benedict XVI in Rome in 2006. The Supreme Court of Canada ruled that Mike Ward's jokes about the young disabled singer did not violate the Charter of Rights and Freedoms, that it did not violate the boy's right to dignity and equality. The judgment pitted the right to freedom of expression against the right to dignity and equality. Without condoning the cruelty of Ward's remarks ironizing about the young singer's appearance, we believe that this acid humour was basically innocuous. The story shows how we are now seeing more and more radical positions on freedom of expression, and increasing volatility in the concomitant points of view.

# CHAPTER 5
# CONTRAST AND IRONY

**C**ontrast is the opposition between two elements that is accentuated by putting them side by side. Underlining this contrast with exaggeration generates a comic effect.

Contrast can make people laugh at everyday life. A sudden noise interrupting a deep silence, especially if it is the forced silence of a church or a performance hall, unfailingly provokes laughter. A fat lady walking with a tiny dog can be the source of giggles. So too, a very small partner in a couple with a partner of immense size, especially if the little one is a man and the big one is a woman, can draw laughter. In fact, a contrast, doubled by an inversion, is even funnier. "If Leonardo discovered that the combination of the beautiful with the ugly intensifies the effects of mimicry, Bruegel was probably the first to extend these effects to the whole human body. Since then, the opposition of contrasts, big and small, fat and thin, has never ceased to produce a disconcerting impression" (Hoffmann, 1957).

## WHAT'S SO FUNNY?

I. Pieter Bruegel, *The Fat Kitchen*, engraving, 1563.

II. Pieter Bruegel, *The Thin Kitchen*, engraving, 1563.

Pieter Bruegel the Elder (1525–1569), one of the most important artists of the Renaissance, had the genius, in his two antithetical engravings *The Fat Kitchen* and *The Thin Kitchen*, to extend the contrast from faces and silhouettes to all the household objects surrounding fat and thin characters. Then, the artist plays on anthropomorphism with objects surrounded by human forms. In this case, the artist extends the mimicry of forms or "homotype," to humans, using the resemblance of forms that some animals have developed to blend into their environment, a resemblance protecting them from predators. Bruegel creates a picture with human qualities that can be seen rubbing off on objects, sinking into them, impregnating them with their substance. This makes the objects become almost alive, populating the space with their presence. The contrast in this case is amplified as in an echo.

III. Evelyn Lambart, *The Town Mouse and the Country Mouse*, animation film, ©NFB, 1980.

"The Town Mouse and the Country Mouse" is one of Aesop's famous *Fables*. Hundreds of other versions of this tale have been written and played, from Aesop (circa 600 BCE) and Horace (c. 60 BCE) to La Fontaine (17th Century). One of the first women to animate, produce and direct for the NFB, Evelyn Lambart (1914-1999), gave a touch of poetry and humour to that fable animated with paper figures. In this fable, the opposition between the two lifestyles is complete: one likes the country's calm and frugality, the other prefers the stress and opulent eateries of the city. The moral of the story is that the country mouse is the wiser one, setting the myth of the purity of nature against the perversions of town life. As well, there is a subtext to this story, reversing the propositions, in a collision between these two lifestyles. The simple life may well be spartan, contrasted with the sumptuous life, its gastronomic excesses and more lively pastimes. This tale is such a well-known one that it has become an everyday icon.

The contrasts of two heroes is almost a cliché of humorous discourse, whether in ancient comedy, classical comedy or more recently, in comic cinema, cartoons and comics.

*Laurel and Hardy* (1927-1951) by Stan Laurel and Oliver Hardy, shorts and full-length movies by diverse directors and producers. The brilliant twosome of American comic cinema, a British-American team, was formed in 1927 during the silent era, and produced 107 films in a joint career that lasted until 1950. Corpulent Hardy (1892-1957) took the lead, while lanky Laurel (1890-1965) was the naïve blunderer. Their gags were dotted with gaffes and their gestural comedy used slapstick and rapid clownish jumps.

## WHAT'S SO FUNNY?

> To accentuate the contrast, Laurel's hair was short but he kept it long and curly on top, creating the impression of a mophead. On the contrary, Hardy's hair seemed pasted on. Their physical attributes reinforced personality traits.

The contrast plays out on all levels, and each element plays into the whole. Here is the eternal duo of the strong and the weak, and according to your own sensibility, you will identify with one or the other. You can imagine being the first, then the second. This back-and-forth game is a unique opportunity to analyze from the inside the forces at play in the seizure of power and, on the other hand, in submission and abandonment.

Hergé, *Tintin's Adventures* (1929–1976, 23 albums).

> Drawn by the Belgian Hergé (George Rémi, 1907-1983) and published weekly first in the *Journal Tintin, Tintin* brought his readers, young and old, from all around the world, incredible adventures which have not aged a day so many years after their inception. The pure and ever brilliant Tintin, with his angelic face and stable character, links up with his friend Captain Haddock, whose persona is crude, choleric and alcoholic. When Haddock is not there, Tintin by himself is a deadly bore, except when he is accompanied by his dog Snowy, forming with his playful dog a second contrasting couple. Snowy often acts like a disobedient child, who is nevertheless prone to remorse or self-doubt. Sometimes, Snowy seems torn between his inner demon and his inner angel. Then, Tintin's parental figure appears and scolds him. In these situations, Tintin takes on the role of the superego, bonding with the reader who can identify with the misbehaving little dog.

Here, the contrast is above all mental, with the reader inclined to side with one of the two characters. Systematic repetition is the funny element in the contrastive situations presented, like an eternal refrain. Clearly this comic strain is as old as comedy itself. The contrasting comic pairs form a core of characters who inspire the laughter that the house of comedy is built on. The contrast of forms, frequent in caricature, often corresponds to a contrast of characters, suggesting an outline in the first degree wants our silhouette to reflect our soul. Which means that an ugly character is bad and a beautiful person is kind. Which fortunately is not true in reality. There is a sort of complementarity in the contrasting couples as if, together, they could form a kind of total superhuman. Laughter flows from the spark between them when the two touch. The town mouse alone doesn't make you laugh. On its own, it is trite, common.

Uderzo and Goscinny, *The Adventures of Asterix*, (1961–2024, 40 albums)

# MIRA FALARDEAU

Another contrasting couple that embodies a universal dream is *Asterix the Gaul*. Asterix and his friend Obelix were born in France in Pilote magazine in 1959 from the pen of Albert Uderzo (1927-2020), scripted by René Goscinny (1926-1977). The series has been translated into one hundred and eleven languages. The saga of *Asterix*, this little Gallic hero, takes place in 50 BC where, with the help of his obese friend Obelix, he continually defeats the Roman armies who want to invade their village. *Asterix* is this little one who wins against all odds, thanks to his superhuman powers acquired by a magic potion and whom every child dream of being like. Obelix, for his part, is the opposite of his friend: he is a big fat fellow mostly interested in eating delectable fat boars just out of the roasting pan, who then sends the Romans into the air with a simple wave of his hand, which is so powerful because of the famous magic potion into which he fell when he was a child. But the numerous allusions to the world of political strategy through puns with the Latin language reach more adults than children, to the great delight of older readers.

Contrast freezes uneven situations, highlights differences by accentuating them. This process lends itself to social criticism as well, which explains the success of cinematic works (animated films, comic films and TV series,) focused on contrasting characters who can cavort endlessly on this comedic canvas.

"*The Fat and the Lean,*" short film, dir. Roman Polanski with Polanski and André Katelbach, France, 1961.

The young director Polanski (Raymond Thierry Liebling, 1933- ) casts himself as a skinny young servant, playing a flute and drum and eager to serve an obese master sitting in the meadow surrounding his home. As the pace of the music accelerates, the young man seems both delighted to serve and on the verge of exhaustion. The poor emaciated servant ends up chained, like a dog on a leash. In one of his very first films, Polanski here paints a dark satire on the inequality of opportunities compounded by the horrors of war, adding Beckett-like accents of the absurd. Stark and almost desperate, the contrast serves here in a cynical critique of injustice and the extremes forced on the poor of this world.

In the same way, the contrast of forms and characters responds to a contrast of movements and actions. From one extreme to the other, the two contrasting characters are exaggerated opposites of each other. If the large character does one thing, the small one will do the opposite. In their run-ins, which to the delight of the public will be frequent, each will stick stubbornly to their position. If one favors calm and negotiation, the other will scream and be confrontational. This is also the source of their humour: their excesses are accentuated by this friction. The Latin proverb "*In medio stat virtus*" holds that virtue is found in the middle, not the extremes. But in comic

# WHAT'S SO FUNNY?

language, the source of laughter is in the extremes. And where are the extremes in any contrasting pair? Opposite ends, of course.

## Irony or saying the opposite

Irony is a subtle form of criticism. As you read or watch, you are invited to side with or oppose the position of the writer or artist. This makes your reading active in the sense that, first of all, you must fully grasp the difference between what is said and what is unsaid. Then, you take a mental path to follow or not follow the argument of the critique. You have the choice between what has been said and what has not been said.

William Shakespeare, *The Taming of the Shrew*, comedy
in five acts (1593), Act IV, scene 5.

Shakespeare has written here a play inserted inside another play, therefore put into a mise en abyme, recounting the romance between Katharina, who pretends to hate men, and Petruchio, who wants to seduce her, in a masterpiece of contrasts and role reversals. Katharina has a strong temper and she doesn't want to be fooled. Petruchio is going to make fun of her by making her almost mad with his contrary views: if she says it's hot, he's going to say the opposite, and so on. She does the same with him. The fact that men played female roles in Shakespearean theater would have made the story even more hilarious for people of that period. When Petruchio begins the "taming" of his new wife, Katharina, he decides to disagree with everything she says just to see how far she will go and to force her to finally agree with him. The result is totally absurd and funny. If you read the scene between the lines, you can see a critique of male-female relationships and how ridiculous confrontations start out. When everyone sticks his position, the contradictions become even more preposterous. Shakespeare in his great humanity shows here the most ridiculous and absurd starting point of most couple's quarrels.

A public road.

*Enter PETRUCHIO, KATHARINA, HORTENSIO, and Servants*

PETRUCHIO: Come on, in God's name, once more toward
our father's.
Good Lord, how bright and goodly shines
the moon!

KATHARINA: The moon? The sun. It is not moonlight now.

# MIRA FALARDEAU

PETRUCHIO: I say it is the moon that shines so bright.

KATHARINA: I know it is the sun that shines so bright.

PETRUCHIO: Now, by my mother's son, and that's myself,
It shall be moon, or star, or what I list,
Or ere I journey to your father's house.
Go on, and fetch our horses back again.
Evermore crossed and crossed; nothing but
crossed!

HORTENSIO (To Katharina): Say as he says, or we shall
never go.

KATHARINA: Forward, I pray, since we have come so far,

And be it moon, or sun, or what you please;

An if you please to call it a rush candle,

Henceforth I vow it shall be so for me.

PETRUCHIO: I say it is the moon.

KATHARINA: I know it is the moon.

PETRUCHIO: Nay, then you lie. It is the blessed sun.

KATHARINA: Then, God be blest, it is the blessed sun:
But sun it is not when you say it is not,
And the moon changes even as your mind.
What you will have it named, even that it is,
And so it shall be so for Katharina.

Many great contemporary writers use irony with finesse, some making it their trademark. David Lodge (1935-), a British writer, laughs shamelessly at the university world in *Changing Places* (1975) and *Small World* (1984), at the business world in *Nice Work* (1988), or the world of television in *Therapy* (1995). Each of these comic works, delights in the virtuosity of satirizing these self-glorifying constructs. And then there is the Franco-Czech author Milan Kundera (1929–2023). The titles of his first two novels, with love as the main theme, *The Joke* (1967) and *Laughable Loves* (1969), offer us clues as to where he is going. The list of major authors who use irony as the main driver would be long indeed.

## WHAT'S SO FUNNY?

Yoni Brenner, "Meanwhile, in Kiev", *The New Yorker*, October 14, 2019, p.33.

President of Ukraine Volodymyr Zelensky had a phone conversation with President of United States Donald Trump, Official Web Site of Volodymyr Zelensky, July 25, 2019.

*Scene: Kiev, July 25, 2019. A conference room in the Mariyinsky Palace. Volodymyr Zelensky, the newly elected president, stands with his ministers. The President of the United States has just hung up.*

President Zelensky: O.K. That was weird. That was weird, right?

*(Murmurs of assent: "Yes". "Very." "Super weird." There is a long pause.)*

Yermak: Are we positive it was him?

Prystaiko: It sounded like him.

Maliuska: It could have been Alec Baldwin.

Yermak: Or Fallon. Fallon does a good one.

Yulia, the President's private secretary: It was a secure diplomatic line, sir. From the White House.

Zelensky *(sighing)*: Too bad. I've always wanted to meet Baldwin.

> Here, in this ironic article signed by American scenarist Yoni Brenner, what is comic is that the president of Ukraine, instead of speaking with the real Trump, would ultimately have preferred to speak with the "fake Trump", who happens to be Alec Baldwin, a recognized humorist, Zelensky's own métier before he was elected president. The incredible televised performance of Alec Baldwin as Trump, on Saturday Night Live broadcasts in 2017, is a conspicuous example of "the verisimilitude of false realty", with irony piercing the rigid shell of appearance, to show the interiority, or the sidereal void, of the mocked character. This indirect tribute to Zelensky's former profession is also an acknowledgment of the fact that irony can be more effective than the plain truth in depicting people realistically and highlighting their flaws.

Since the rise of the internet, humorous webzines have emerged, some specializing in fake news. Obviously, some of these sites also privilege the use of irony. And the crazy aspect of all this is that some

## MIRA FALARDEAU

readers are taken in by pseudo-news posted on Facebook and other social networks by sinister operatives who gull the gullible. Those who are taken in then pass on such distortions of reality to their friends who get caught in turn, and the cycle doesn't end unless some skeptic is heard blowing the whistle on such fraudulent claims. The same is true of a certain type of irony in internet memes, as we saw in the preceding chapter. With memes, one more step is taken in the mixing of genres, as well as in the mixing of language levels.

# CHAPTER 6
# INVERSION

**I**nversion is a figure of permutation whereby the relative positions of two things or two persons are reversed.

The Feast of Fools, a carnivalesque celebration in which students and young clerics played a role-reversal game with high-ranking ecclesiastics (circa 1200–1450)

The ritual merrymaking called La Fête des Fous was organized at the end of December or the beginning of January in most cities and in monasteries, as well. Within consecrated walls, a fools' pope was elected, often a child deacon, invested with a host of papal attributes. Everybody sang burlesque canticles overflowing with puns and ribald songs and drank lots of wine while the actual priests would ascend up to the altar to fill up on pork delicacies and drinks. Then, all these fetching drunken people would surge through city streets, climb onto garbage carts and throw the contents down at delighted onlookers. After the festivities, all the members of the clergy, along with the students, would resume their rightful roles (Minois, 2000). Contrary to what one might think, this celebration was absolutely not improvised but highly codified; its ceremonial procedures are detailed in the manual L'office de la fête des fous, written by Pierre de Corbeil, Archbishop of Sens, around 1200. Initially forbidden but subsequently tolerated, these ritual festivities flourished for several centuries not only in France but also in Belgium and elsewhere in Europe. They were definitively proscribed in 1444 and again in 1519.

We can feel the link connecting these games of role reversal between low-ranking and eminent men of the Church and those of Greek peasants who disguised themselves as women to run in the streets, quite drunk, during the celebrations dedicated to Dionysus. In both

## MIRA FALARDEAU

cases, we are witnessing not spontaneous but rather ritual laughter, in the context of a religious rite (Ballagrida, 2006). The inversion of social status which participants engaged in during these festivities at once popular and religious unfolded in a prescribed pattern. Everyone would release pent-up energy and tension, would open up a lived experience of temporary chaos, then return to the established order.

Such games find their way into the theatre. There may not be so great a distance, after all, between the Greek audience who enjoyed the mocking of the high and mighty in Aristophanes' comedies and the African commoners who would hurl insults at their king-to-be. Indeed, in Greece, "the gods were treated like the political rulers of the city" (Ballagrida, 2006). The schema of the inverted world is therefore a powerful comic spring, whether the inversion is between races, between social classes, between age groups or between the sexes. Let us remember *The Assemblywomen* of Aristophanes (see Chapter 1) in which women take on men's social roles, delighting the public.

Moreover, social inversion constitutes a powerful way to facilitate the acceptance of the different roles enacted. In Aristophanes' *The Frogs*, the playwright praises intemperance and obscene songs. Ritual obscenity in the theater, episodes of collective laughter, were experienced as great catharses, a sort of group liberation, just like dreams freeing the individual from their anxieties. The traces of ritual insults found in Africa when a king accedes to the throne enable him to understand his subjects, since he put himself in their shoes and had to laugh with them.

To see oneself in other people's shoes helps release tension through laughter. This is precisely the most common function of role reversal. Concerning private as well as public interactions, inversion plays on the binary nature of relationships. Furthermore, this polarity is perfect to express irony about social relationships. Inversion can be used explicitly or implicitly.

Understanding this logic, Bergson speaks as follows, about reversal, in his chapter on situational comedy: "Imagine certain characters in a certain situation: you will get a comic scene by having the situation turned around and the roles switched." He continues, "But it is not even necessary to perform the two symmetrical scenes before our eyes. One can only show one scene, as long as he is sure we are thinking of the other" (Bergson, 1901).

## WHAT'S SO FUNNY?

In comedy, the game of inversion between activities of two social groups has been utilized by generations of artists. The refinement of this figure and of its multiple uses has made it a favorite process in popular imagery and in boulevard theater.

> Beaumarchais, *The Marriage of Figaro,* comedy in five acts, (1778).
>
> In the pre-revolutionary latter part of the 18th century, in front of the intelligent and cunning valet Figaro stands the tricked nobleman, Count Almaviva. The subtlety with which the great French playwright Pierre Augustin Caron de Beaumarchais (1732-1799) inverted his characters' attitudes is exemplary, especially considering he did so with the avowed aim of criticizing the nobility's powerful position.

At the turn of the 20$^{th}$ century, this kind of comic gesture first permeated the world of entertainment and theater before it swept into films and cartoons, then comics. The reversal of gestures quite naturally became one of the great comic forces of the 7$^{th}$ and 9$^{th}$ arts. "The archetype of a humorous drawing is certainly the protean and almost eternal image of the world upside down" (Melot, 1975). The process of comic reversal provided tools for the portrayal of class warfare as well as of the feminist struggle in subsequent centuries. The figure of inversion will naturally become the privileged figure of feminist discourse, as we will see.

I. *Les réformes du ménage (*Household Reforms), Épinal images, Fabrique de Pellerin, 1890.

**Translation:**

1. Women will join business and politics.
2. Women will go to the tavern.
3. Young ladies will seduce gentlemen and convey declarations.
4. At the ball, gentlemen will wait until they are invited to dance.
5. The ladies will choose their husbands.
6. These gentlemen will not have the right to refuse.
7. This is how we will deal with boys who refuse to marry.
8. Only ladies will be able to take up arms.

This work takes the form of a series of prints where various situations are simply inverted with men taking the place of women and vice-versa, evoked by very stereotypical engravings. The chronicler of the late 19th century seems to say: the excesses of social transformation would lead to this mess, if people changed places, in fact men, would go crazy (no). Just as people in ancient Greece or in the Middle Ages amused themselves by taking the place of their rulers or the priests in the pulpit during a carnival or a Fools' Feast, they now laughed at women of the type from *Commedia dell'arte* and boulevard theater who had fun wearing trousers and running businesses while men washed the dishes. Not only is it a matter of making men, as a social group, think about thankless and repetitive tasks devolved on their sweethearts but also of projecting women spectators and readers onto the "better side" of society while the entertainment lasted.

At the dawn of the 20th century, the game of role reversal between man and woman was already beginning to have a different, almost premonitory flavor. But our evaluation in the 2020s is obviously very different, since many of these gender-neutral roles are now taken for granted, which adds to the humour of the reading.

II. Albéric Bourgeois, *Les aventures de Timothée* (The adventures of Timothée), *La Patrie*, Montreal, January 30, 1904.

# WHAT'S SO FUNNY?

**Translation:**

> Box 1: Timothy — No one can resist my charms.
> Box 2: T. -Good heavens, what a pretty woman!
> Box 3: T. — My beautiful little one… allow me…
> Box 4: The lady – About face right!
> Box 5: The lady -Ten-Hup!
> Box 6: L. — A little exercise is great for your health!
> Timothy — On the contrary!

The Quebec cartoonist Albéric Bourgeois (1876–1962) is presenting here a role reversal typical of *commedia dell'arte*. This strip is really attacking the stereotype of the strong man. By reversing the two propositions: man/strong and woman/weak, we obtain the following: man/weak and woman/strong. The immediate comic effect of these propositions comes from the immense evocative potential of its irony, which can be interpreted in diverse ways.

He stages the theme of the shrew using a variant of reversal. Normally, the shrew is an ageless woman with a graceless physique and willful demeanor. Bourgeois has retained the shrew's psychological characteristics, but, being a connoisseur of popular theater techniques, he decides to surprise readers with a lady of fetching appearance. The beau will be astonished because how can one expect not only masculine but moreover military behavior from such an elegant person?

The comic effect arises from the surprise created by the contrast between the man's expected attitude and the lady's reaction. But also, from the virile vigor with which the elegant lady makes the dandy twirl in three successive takes, thanks to the cane she snatches from him. We cannot ignore the phallic symbol of the cane so powerfully seized. She is now in control! Then, she violently knocks the poor fellow down as his bruises and torn clothes attest in the last box.

The text supports the point and gives even more color to the role reversal. In the first three boxes, the flirt attempts to lull the woman with a melody of sweet words: "My charms, pretty woman, beautiful little one." In the last three boxes, there is a contrasted disruption caused by his female attacker's military commands: "About face, march right, Attention!" ironic here because the poor fellow's gestures are completely involuntary and unworthy of a drill formation. In these orders similar to those of a master corporal, the mechanical side largely predominates, adding to the wackiness of the situation. Let us mention that this strip was the first French-language comic strip, long before the Belgian and French comic strips, as we discovered during our research.

As we would expect, if male authors were the first to take hold of the role reversal process, with the advent of feminism, female authors in turn would be able to ironize on social inequality using this humorous figure.

72

With the rising underground and the countercultural press, a new challenge awaited women comedic artists. During the 1970s and 1980s, the women's liberation movement coincided in the United States with the birth of underground comics; one of their characteristics was total freedom of language be it visual or textual. A large number of *fanzines*, magazines sold more or less discreetly in various parallel outlets, were born and died out after a few issues, including some resolutely feminist fanzines created by women. They approached women's issues by making extensive use of inversion.

III. Nicole Hollander, "*That woman must be on drugs*", St-Martin's Press, 1981.

Nicole Hollander (1939- ), an American artist and comics publisher, became a champion of relentlessly passive-aggressive protest. Here, Hollander responds with almost elegant irony to the sexist comments of her interlocutor. The vulgarity of the speech should not prevent one from feeling the weariness of the artist. The first degree of the dialogue is a type of retaliation: an eye for an eye and a tooth for a tooth. More deeply, by turning the tide and flipping a scathing barb at the man, the woman underscores the futility, but also the devastating aspect of many male remarks about women's physical appearance. Here, it is also necessary to underline her ironic vision of the opposition in the male imagination between women's beauty and intelligence, a contradiction most damaging to harmonious relationships between men and women!

The women artists of the first feminist wave found themselves stuck between their very legitimate aspirations to free themselves from the constraints of previous eras and the pornographic and ultraviolent delirium of their colleagues. It should not be forgotten that a whole movement of male underground artists took pride in representing women in unsightly and often humiliating positions or, surprisingly, endowed with all-masculine warlike prowess.

IV. Sue Dewar, "*Good Lord, Ethel*", *Ottawa Sun*, May 16, 1997.

The Canadian cartoonist Sue Dewar (1949- ) is probably the only woman who has held the position of editorial cartoonist in Canada. At present, Dewar draws for the

*Toronto Sun* and the *Winnipeg Sun*. In this cartoon, she is ironic about diverse perceptions of the reciprocal corpulence of two spouses, as if there were a double standard! Obviously, the addition of flabby and unaesthetic flesh adds to the ridiculousness of the scene, as showing off half-naked on beaches is usually part of a process of exalting beauty! In a meeting we had in 2020, Dewar recalled that every time the news allowed her, she took a stand for women. But sometimes the interpretation can play tricks: addressing her as Mr. Dewar, a reader complained about one of her cartoons regarding sex. When he found out she was a woman, he understood the different point of view!

There has been a clear return to this type of discourse in recent years, but trivialized and more generalized. Whether in video games or in films inspired thereby or in fantasy-style comics, artistic works abound where women's roles are reduced to the incarnation of male readers' fantasies but with men's strange gestures and inversion of attitudes. Watching these muscular and intrepid creatures, one has the impression of seeing men with female faces and busty breasts, just like the men playing women from ancient theatre up to classical comedy. A thorough study of generously-shaped supergirls drawn by male artists would be most enlightening as to this strange role reversal, but it remains to be done.

Inversions concerning children and parents are also very revealing in these times of social upheaval.

Françoise Ménager « *L'école des parents* » (Parents' School), *Fmagazine*, Paris, Sept. 19, 1979.

**Action:** In this twelve-box silent comic, we can see a mother in tears on her daughter's first day of school, hugging her and almost unable to let her go into the school. Finally, the little girl frees herself from the arms of her overprotective mother, pulls her by the skirt, then pushes her along to another building and up the steps into the "Parents' School". As she leaves, the girl says good-bye with a laugh.

There is a certain visionary aspect in this strip by French cartoonist Francoise Ménager (1949- ) «L'école des parents» (Parents' School). Published forty years ago, it prefigures present-day lack of authority. The massive feminine workforce outside the home is redefining the primary role of women in patriarchal society, the role of mother. Indeed, the little girl, child-empress, is the winner of the story. She has freed herself from the hold of her mother's suffocating love, from her "mother-prison".

There is a displacement here because the mother seems to imagine she was about to imprison her child by bringing her to school. In fact, the little girl is actually laughing

## WHAT'S SO FUNNY?

at her prank, because it is she who locks up her mother, forcing her to learn a new role. In this mother/child role reversal, the mother's attitude is being questioned.

Criticizing a society where the reign of the only child has given birth to a new generation of child dictators, this satire concludes that by wanting to perform too well, the new generation of parents has undoubtedly made as many mistakes as the previous cohort. Is it better to exert too much authority or, on the other side, allow for too much laxity? The mother, with a slumped back and discouraged expression, watches her young one go off, letting her cut the symbolic cord herself. The comic inversion in this context can represent the permutation between the traditional mother's role, transmitted to us by our own mothers or by the family's female clan — aunts, grandmothers and others — and the new woman's role, where everything has to be reinvented. A second-degree analysis of this type of inversion consists in the conferral of the new role to the girl-child, in a shift which produces: role of mother = my own mother, role of daughter = role of the new woman.

By reversal, the youngster becomes the mother of her mother, teaching her how to be a mother since she can no longer see a social beacon. This scenario occurs regularly in a radically transformed society like ours. While the profession of parent, more precisely of mother, was learned by following the example in large families or communities, such as villages or parishes, the now lonely mother of the nuclear family in large urban centres could well be tempted by a parents' school, considering the enormous task of being "superwomen".

The inversion of forms can also help a humorous discourse deal with the important social changes generated by immigration.

| V. Martine Chartrand, *Black Soul*, Glass painting animation, ©NFB, 2001.

## MIRA FALARDEAU

Martine Chartrand (1962- ) is an artist of Haitian origin from Montreal, a cinema animator at the National Film Board of Canada where she specializes in glass painting. *Black Soul* is a wooden statuette used by a Haitian grandmother to illustrate, for her grandson, the history of Black people in Quebec. As the grandmother speaks, drawings printed on her dress begin to move and narrate their saga. By metonymy, the grandmother carries the story through fluid images sliding into one another in successive metamorphoses to the rhythm of music evolving from gospel to jazz. At the end, the Black boy sculpts Black Soul's silhouette in the snow, as his little Quebecois friends circle around him. Thus, the primordial mother, a brown wooden doll, hard and warm, has become an ice sculpture, white, malleable and cold. Such an inversion of symbols in a chiasm seems like the child's echo of Gilles Vigneault's song: "My country, it's not a country, it is winter, (...) My song, it's not a song, it is snow". In becoming integrated into this society, the child has exchanged the image of an ancestral woman for another, equally beautiful but corresponding to his new country. He has expressed what he carried deep inside but has now shaped it for the years to come. Therefore, by reverse reflection, the tradition conveyed by an old woman's figure becomes the future in the hands of the boy.

Humorous inversion is often used by minorities, or by groups that feel aggrieved, such as women, people of color or those at the bottom of the social ladder. The inversion acts like a mirror. For example: "This is how I would feel in her place", or "How does she feel when she does this to me"? Or, its reverberation: "This is how she must feel when I do this to her", "How would I feel if I did this to her"?

Fundamentally, the humorous role-reversal figure invites you to put yourself in the other person's shoes in order to understand him or her, apprehend their reality and ultimately, come to live together in mutual tolerance, in another inner self. This process is about exaggerating positions, looking at them with a wacky vision to better understand the strategic points. It's really about making fun of a system to subvert it. Humorous role reversal, whichever element is reversed, is a powerful social game. Humour, beneath its light exterior, plays into the depths of our subconscious, where our social mythologies are created. For what purpose? To make people laugh in order to defuse, transcend and transform.

# CHAPTER 7
# REPETITION, ACCUMULATION, GRADATION

**R**epetition is the recurrence of the same word, same gesture or same action.

Repetition is the accumulation of identical elements, like the bursts of hiccup that keep on coming. And in fact, in everyday life, someone with the hiccups makes others laugh, as if their silhouette, temporarily dehumanized, obeyed an internal mechanism, like an automaton. And this is exactly the feeling that takes hold of us when we watch a comedy: the feeling that life, all of a sudden, is functioning like a mechanism. That it is no longer governed by sensible and informed decisions, but by a kind of machine. This is Bergson's famous: "mechanical plastered onto the human". "We laugh whenever a human being gives us the impression of a thing "(Bergson, 1901). What student hasn't laughed out loud when a teacher who was distracted or embarrassed kept repeating the same word, such as "so" or "well"?

Molière (1622–1673), *The Tartuffe or the Impostor* (*Tartuffe ou l'imposteur*), comedy in five acts, (1664, 1669), Act I, scene 5.

DORINE: The day before yesterday, Madame had a fever
until the evening,

# MIRA FALARDEAU

With a headache strange to conceive.
ORGON: And Tartuffe?

DORINE: Tartuffe! He is doing wonderfully,
Big and fat, fresh complexion and vermilion
mouth.

ORGON: The poor man!

DORINE: In the evening, she had a great disgust,
And could not, at supper, touch anything at all,
So cruel was her headache!

ORGON: And Tartuffe?

DORINE: He supped, just himself, in front of her;
And very devoutly he ate two partridges,
With half a chopped leg of lamb.

ORGON — The poor man!"

Orgon, a rich man admiring Tartuffe, a pharisee, has become so gullible under the influence of the hypocrite Tartuffe, that he goes so far as to host him at his home and finds himself totally subjugated by him. In this scene, he replies successively "And Tartuffe" and "The poor man" twice, for a total of four repetitions, in response to the maid. In fact, Dorine alternates the narration of the misfortunes overwhelming the poor Mariane (sic) and of the well-being of Tartuffe, in sharp contrast to the logical response he should give: to pity Mariane and to ignore Tartuffe. He exaggerates with his reply pitying Tartuffe.

It is said (Raeders, 1947) that this expression was inspired by a real event: at the time of Molière, a monk is supposed to have exclaimed "The poor man" upon hearing the story of a famous priest's excesses. Louis XIV, in turn, supposedly repeated it when he heard the story of a banquet given by the Archbishop of Paris. It should be noted that the king had approved the first version of *Tartuffe* of 1664 in which Molière openly mocked prelates. But thereafter, Molière had to water down his speech, and gave Tartuffe a more secular look!

In short, his scathing criticism is accompanied by redundant mannerisms. Orgon's insensitivity to Mariane's ailments is accentuated by the repetition of phrases punctuating the exchange. His coldness dehumanizes him a little more with each reply. You could say, too, that his stupidity takes him further and further away from the normal feelings he should be experiencing! In fact, this process, even if it seems to stall the action, drives the comic point home a little deeper with each line. Indeed, Molière is a fervent user of repetition.

## WHAT'S SO FUNNY?

It is interesting to note that we have just seen above the confirmation that, during the Renaissance era, comedies had to be approved by the king. We saw the same process with Rabelais, who was "protected"; otherwise, he would not have been able to say a quarter of what he did. In fact, it was necessary to be shielded by those in power to benefit from a certain freedom of expression. Which was not given to everyone, and which could be considered a privilege. The privilege for everybody of saying what we think through humour is in fact quite recent in the history of our democracies.

Prohias, *Spy vs Spy, Mad Magazine*, # 60, 1961.

Action: In the very first page of this series, the two antagonists have a friendly meeting in a cafe. They serve each other a coffee. Pretending to drink it, each one surreptitiously pours his coffee on the floor, suspecting the other of wanting to poison him. Under the table, two cats are lapping up the contents of the two cups. The two cats fall on their backs and die as the two Spies get up and politely shake hands before parting.

First signed by Antonio Prohias (1921–1998), a Cuban author who hardly spoke English, which explains the speechless gags, *Spy vs Spy* lasted sixty years with six different authors in the American humour magazine *Mad Magazine*. The base of the storyline was relatively simple. In a weekly sequence, two spies with identical faces and profiles, except that one is dressed in white and the other in black, clash regularly, with a final turnaround. There are several types of repetition in these strips. First of all, a visual one: the two characters are identical. Apart from the color of their clothes, which differentiates them, each one is a carbon copy of the other, with their typical pointy noses and ample medieval cloaks. Another kind of repetition is narrative: each episode uses the same structure. It is always the same scenario of the would-be trapper's getting caught in his own trap.

Generally speaking, the pattern is as follows: one tries to trap the other, but the punch line is that it is the first who gets trapped. Or perhaps no one is trapped, as in this very first strip. The funny thing is that there is no winner, but an alternation depending on the episodes: first one wins, and then the other, and sometimes both, as above. But it is the repetition of the leitmotif which creates the comic effect, since the reader knows the outcome but laughs even more with each episode, as if knowing the outcome made the gag even funnier, and not the reverse, which would have been more logical. Spy versus Spy, therefore, has been an uninterrupted refrain for more than sixty years of a totally jackass gag between two entities almost devoid of humanity, who never die or

# MIRA FALARDEAU

suffer despite all the calamities endured and which are still making us laugh: this is comic repetition incarnate.

Repetition operates as one of the fundamental springs of burlesque, whether in comic cinema or in cartoons, in the venerable tradition of commedia dell'arte.

Chuck Jones, *"Road Runner"* in the *Looney Tunes* series, Warner Brothers (24 cartoons were made from 1949 to 1964).

Created by the American animator Chuck Jones (1912–2002), one of the most striking examples of redundancy of gestures is undoubtedly that famous Road Runner revived later with other signatures. The basic scheme is simplistic: the coyote chases Road Runner down a desert road and, using either elaborate or unsophisticated machines, all supplied by the mock-iconic ACME company, he tries to catch him but always misses the mark. The flatness of the scenario is vivified by laws of incremental absurdity. For example, Road Runner very rarely obeys the law of gravity. Coyote and Road Runner can sometimes pass through the backdrop of the cartoon. Road Runner can abruptly stop his plunge into the void without falling. Coyote can crash into a boulder at full speed without being injured. The irresistible comedy of these short sequences comes from the repetition of the impossible feats of the two antagonists, seasoned with the improbable "Beep-Beep" of Road Runner, cartoon after cartoon. The perfectly oiled mechanism of the animal chases in this almost abstract setting belies the theory of laughter in the face of surprise, because here we find precisely the opposite. We laugh despite knowing what's going to happen. In fact, we know what's going to happen, but not how.

When comic speech presents us with three or more elements or events that are completely identical, our reason jumps. The chance of this happening in reality is slim! "This is because living life shouldn't repeat itself" (Bergson, 1901). Hence our burst of laughter. And if I am a humorist or a cartoonist, what better way to emphasize the cruelty or the lack of emotion in people or institutions I want to criticize than to dehumanise them? To show how like machines they are, cold and repetitive?

## Accumulation

Two other processes related to repetition are **accumulation** and **gradation**. These three processes are quantitative processes, playing primarily on exaggeration. Take accumulation. In everyday life, one effortlessly thinks of a teenager's bedroom, or an untidy wardrobe where all the objects are piled up into a jumble. Nothing really funny. But all it takes is for a stacked object to fall on the person opening the wardrobe door or for someone to go belly-up sliding on a rolling object camouflaged by the mess for the laughter to burst forth. When the accumulation of elements due to chance provokes an unexpected gesture or behavior, surprise gives way to a comic effect.

Especially in drawings, not only does the jumble of objects or actions strike the imagination, but all these lines describing objects, persons or actions seem to have an existence of their own. It is as if the whole exerted a special force greater than the sum of its parts. We often say "Strength in numbers".

I. Lynda Barry, "Two questions", from *What It Is?*
© Lynda Barry 2013. Used with permission from Drawn & Quarterly.

For the American underground artist Lynda Barry (1956- ) the comic use of accumulation is the mainspring, but in a psychological context. Here, the entanglement of ideas is symbolized by an entanglement of lines. Barry stands in the field of underground discourse which is marked by exaggeration in lines, as we have seen. This page may give the illusion of an aimless shambles but its form of discourse is very intimate, which is why it has been chosen. The subject of this work concerns the inevitable questions jostling around in the artist's head when the fertile early years of creativity are spent. But Barry's jam-packed space expresses, above all, a kind of suffocation due to an overabundance of emotions or ideas weighing down their author. "Is it good?" and "Does it suck?" are the two questions. And they spin around in her head, leading to a loss of confidence and doubts about the value of her work. Here, no space is empty: four types of data are piled up on the page: sentences synthesizing her logorrhea, crisscrossing abstract lines that weave a net of squares and twists floating in space, some physical silhouettes evoking first an octopus, perhaps a part of Barry's consciousness and then her self-portrait reading

"Grimm's Fairy Tales", and, finally, words outside dialogues like qualifiers, affixed to rockets, such as "stupid" or "genius" or historical names appearing on book covers: "Freud, Lao Tzu, Greek Mythology." Barry's density of design overlays discourse to evoke thought, and the mass of information does not produce satiety but rather continuity. The fact that levels of meaning intersect without colliding plays on a kind of harmony emerging from the whole, for those who know how to read this kind of comic art. And at the same time, Barry here shouts at us her dismay, her panic at the overflow of emotion represented by comic accumulation, with a juxtaposition of emotions.

This power is intrinsic to the cluster. Like a new being. A new aggregation imposing itself, even if it has no particular shape. In the accumulation, there is a hint of chaos, disruption. In comedic speech, accumulation can be brought on to figure anger or extreme joy. Or quite simply to figure chance or awkwardness. Or the lack of social control: in the representation of collective jubilation, uncontrollable actions stacked on top of each other unleash hilarity in the viewer. An irrational run of mishaps happening to the same person invariably spark hysterical laughter, the comedic type of the jinxed character being the best example.

Posy Simmonds, *Tamara Drew*, graphic novel, Jonathan Cape Publ., 2007.

The British cartoonist Posy Simmonds (1945- ) has made a name for herself with her preferred discourse wherein the levels of language are as if superimposed to give an impression of real-life throbbing within small upper-middle-class country communities, sometimes clashing with the "locals", which she brilliantly depicts in graphic novels. *Tamara Drew*, inspired by Thomas Hardy's famous 19th-century novel *Far from the Madding Crowd*, has been adapted into film, (2010, dir. Stephen Frears), as has *Gemma Bovery* (2014, dir. Anne Fontaine), a work from 1999, a nod to Flaubert's *Madame Bovary*. Simmonds gives shape to female voices in a crossover between generations. Her accumulations are here made up of a set of texts of different natures, newspaper articles — fake, of course — dialogues in real time, posters, talk from the main protagonist who speaks directly to the reader as if she were telling us her story, by commenting on it. For example, we can see in this album, a page of email with address, object and text (p. 66), a number of newspaper clippings with a pseudo pink post-it, complete with name and date (p. 122), a letter with the header of an eminent publisher (p. 97), an extract of a color pulp magazine (p. 85). All of these voices encompass the story like a circular panoramic shot in a film, giving it a deeper life than a simple monochord story. There is also a resonant irony in casting the characters of the story in a "false" media environment, irony derived from the "special effects" of advertising.

# WHAT'S SO FUNNY?

> Moreover, we can see in this abundance of documents surrounding her characters an ironic allusion to the current tendency to give more importance to show-business personalities by accumulating advertisements on all media in the hope of increasing their popularity.

One can undoubtedly speak of accumulation in the case of the numerous compilations of cartoons by this or that cartoonist. Or collections of funny stories. There is a particular kind of phenomenon whereby the more I peruse compilations of comic stories or comic drawings, the more I laugh. It is this very process that makes crowds collapse into laughter when watching the repetitive gags in a funny movie or during stand-up comedy routines so popular nowadays.

Repetition, whether voluntary or not, triggers laughter through its mechanistic aspect. In the same way, many very trendy funny websites currently offer such a smorgasbord of gags that there is a kind of overkill causing customers to laugh until the tears start to flow. Yes, on these websites, I can watch one, two, or more episodes in a row, but even though there is no connection between the various scenes I've just watched, I will end up laughing at the accumulated mass of humour. Somewhat like an overdose. For example, many people love to watch and laugh till satiety at comic sites such as *Funny or Die*, an American site founded in 2006 by comedian Will Ferrell and director Adam McKay. It offers online humorous videos featuring star-system personalities or comic videos filmed by amateurs or professionals, either from real events or invented scenes. A popular vote of "Funny" allows the video to survive on the site while a "Die" vote eliminates it. That said, comic sites are so plentiful it is fruitless to count or name them. They are born and die with such regularity that naming the process suffices to highlight this new face of comic accumulation.

## Gradation

If in accumulation there is stacking, in gradation there is addition, according to a planned pattern. While accumulation can bring together objects or words quite varied in nature, gradation usually presents elements of the same nature, wherein each one interlocks with the previous one.

Edmond Rostand, *Cyrano de Bergerac*, comedy in five acts, (1897), Act 1, scene 4.

# MIRA FALARDEAU

*Cyrano's monologue describing his own nose:*

THE VISCOUNT: No one? But wait! I'll treat him to...
one of my quips! ...

See here!... (*He goes up to Cyrano, who is watching him, and with a conceited air*): Sir, your nose is...hmm...it is...very big!

CYRANO (gravely): Very!

THE VISCOUNT (laughing): Ha!

CYRANO (imperturbably): Is that all?...

THE VISCOUNT: What do you mean?

CYRANO: Ah no! young blade! That was a trifle short!
You might have said at least a hundred things
By varying the tone...like this, suppose, ...

*Aggressive*: 'Sir, if I had such a nose, I'd amputate it!'

*Friendly*: 'When you sup it must annoy you, dipping in your
cup;
You need a drinking-bowl of special shape!'

*Descriptive*: ''Tis a rock! ...a peak! ...a cape!
A cape, forsooth! 'Tis a peninsula!'

The French dramaturg Edmond Rostand (1868–1918) achieved a masterpiece by composing his most famous play in classical, yet so fluid, alexandrines, alternating romantic moments and farcical ones, inspired by commedia dell'arte. Here, at the start of the play, Cyrano, suffering from an inferiority complex because of his ungraceful physique, quips about his own very large nasal appendage, while fighting a sword duel with the suitor of the one he loves in secret. Both grotesque because of his ugliness and heroic because of his courage, he is the very illustration of the lovable and touching romantic hero. This tirade's gradation is built from a spontaneous rhythm that breathes with ever increasing expansion. We think he will stop, but no, he keeps on going and pulls us in. Indeed, the actual tirade lasts another 36 stanzas. Yes, you read that right.

It's the snowball effect. Bergson alludes to this with the example of a comic situation whose pattern is that of a game of dominoes. One situation triggers another, which triggers a third, and so on. The philosopher gives *Don Quixote* as an illustration:

"[...] in certain scenes of *Don Quixote*, for example in the hotel, where a singular chain of circumstances leads the mule driver to strike

## WHAT'S SO FUNNY?

Sancho, who knocks on Maritorne, on which the innkeeper falls, etc. "(Bergson, 1901)".

What is irresistible about these sequences is that viewers are immediately drawn into a whirlwind of cascading laughter where their logical minds are momentarily disconnected. They slip into a world apart, a zany imaginary world. Burlesque comedy, and its sequel, burlesque cinema, play out exactly in this same unreal territory.

Indeed, we can't help feeling a kind of comfort in the recognition of a formula which is repeated time after time. This is repetition squared in the case of series, whether in movies, cartoons, comics or web series. Each sequence repeats to satiety the same string of bad luck or dirty tricks, depending on the point of view. A bit like variations on a theme in baroque music or jazz or like the refrain in song, which gives rhythm to reception by reassuring the audience with its repetitive aspect, in the manner of a pulse.

Even if the word gradation evokes a rise, as if we were gradually climbing the scale of laughter, each step adding to the previous one, in fact, comic gradation is, above all, a descent into hell for the one who is the object of mockery, who undergoes the effects of gradation in comic staging. Or if it's not a descent into hell, at least it's what is called a nightmare sequence. Why are all these things happening to this poor man, to this poor woman, to this poor animal? As to why the laugh numbs the one who is laughing, that is a torturous but unanswered question. This mystery is part of what some have called the "impossible definition of humour" (see Chap. 1). Is it this feeling of superiority, of which Freud speaks, that makes us laugh at someone else's predicament? Is it a big sigh of relief: if this has happened to him or her, perhaps there is less chance that it will happen to me? Bergson tells us that "The comic requires something like a momentary anesthesia of the heart."

*A Fish Called Wanda*, comedy film (dir. Crichton, Great Britain, 1988)

> Roughly speaking, this feature recounts a quarrel in a group of diamond-thieving bandits. The succession of comic events in the film guarantees a succession of individual bursts of laughter that end up morphing into a huge side-splitting wave that bowls you over by its intensity. For instance, the scene at Ken's flat: when the psychopath Otto wants to make Ken reveal where the safety-deposit box is, with the diamonds, by torturing him in eating before his very eyes, one after the other all the little fishes of his beloved aquarium, including the angelfish Wanda, that scene is incredible of zany. It is easy to see that comic repetition operates on several levels at the same time:

## MIRA FALARDEAU

> exaggeration of gesture and action, simplification of narrative patterns, often doubled with inversions and contrasts. Spectators are transported into a totally crazy universe.

The same in *Le dîner de cons* (The Stupid's Dinner, dir. Weber, France, 1998). To see the tax inspector savoring a great wine to which vinegar has been added so that he does not recognize the grand cru, which is in itself an aberration, added to the fact that he finds this wine delicious, and then who learns that his wife is cheating on him with the man he is just controlling is impossible to watch without laughing until exhaustion! "In short, the comedy of repetition in its purest form, far more an amplifier than a generator of comedy, falls under the heading of minimalist art through its simplicity of means and its economy of use to which a sense of just proportion forces it in order to avoid asthenia and boredom. Hence, its very frequent enrichment with equally comical variations or additions: their synergy produces the strength of what I call "comic constellations" (Baudin, 2007). In burlesque cinema, slapstick, or quick visual pranks such as painless whacks with a stick or a cream pie in the face, we truly find the most faithful map of these constellations. Indeed, we laugh at comic repetition, but is it not a defense against the gloomy repetitiveness of assembly-work or of the drudgery of domestic chores?

# CHAPTER 8
# TRANSFERS-ANTHROPOMORPHISM

**A**nthropomorphism is the process by which human forms, gestures, words and behaviors are attributed to animals or objects.

Starting here, all the processes analyzed in the following chapters can be considered as transfers. In other words, we cannot see these things in nature. Obviously, such creatures as talking animals are never found in a state of nature; even if often this would be very practical ...! However, now there are many talking machines, such as GPS, automatic answering machines, talking robots of different kinds and voices generated by AI, but nobody actually knows where all these inventions will take us. Another chapter of human experience is opened with machines with almost human voices, but one thing is sure for the moment: no more humour in these voices.

Chapter after chapter, we shall be exploring our subject from different angles, and our historical walk through each process may cause repetitions. We will certainly bring up Shakespeare, Molière, or Valium on several occasions...But in different ways. The shift from object shapes to human forms with a metaphoric intent is a classic in humour. We can speak of **objectification**, when a person has the shape of an object, or **mechanization**, when the person acts like an object. The forms then seem to have a life of their own, driven by a kind of mechanism.

It is an intrinsic trait of human thought to attribute human characteristics to animals or objects and vice versa. "Childish animism is the tendency to imagine things as alive and purposeful. In infancy, any object that carries out an activity is alive…" (Piaget, 1967). Of course, for children it seems quite normal that animals communicate with each other like humans. It is only as they grow up that they will understand the undersides of these fables and then gradually, the moral nuances conferred by their authors.

Furthermore, symbolic thinking, wherein an object or animal represents a concept or a belief, is as old as humanity itself. In combination with the desire to make people laugh while educating them or criticizing a behavior, this frame of mind generated Aesop's fables, which in turn inspired Lafontaine's, and led to other animal allegories right up to the present day.

*The Grasshopper and the Ant*, extract from Jean de La Fontaine (1668) inspired by Aesop's Fables (6th c. BCE)

> The Ant's not a lender, I must confess. Her heart's far from tender to one in distress. So, she said: "Pray, how passed you the summer, That in winter you come to distress? — "I sang through the summer," Grasshopper said. "But now I am glummer because I've no bread." "So, you sang" sneered the Ant. "That relieves me. Now it's winter. Go dance for your bread!"

In their Fables, Aesop and La Fontaine enjoyed making animals talk to show human qualities and faults, without overlooking the physical traits or typical behaviors of these animals. The rat is smart, the donkey is stupid, the fox is cunning and the grasshopper is happy-go-lucky. But why should the frog be dumber than the ox, as one can see in *The Frog and the Ox*? Sometimes, the correspondences seem totally arbitrary to the 21st- century public; no doubt because we lack references to certain myths going back into the depths of human history and having lasted for millennia in primitive symbolic grammar.

Since the appearance of the first caricature, powerful symbolism has been expressed through transfers of form. For example, as we saw in the first chapter (Ill. III), at the time of theological disputes in early Christianity, Christ himself was shown with a donkey's head; such a picture was discovered scratched on a wall near the Palatine Hill in Rome, probably in a mischievous allusion to the donkey that carried Mary and Jesus, but interpretations vary. Later, in the mid-16th century, we find engravings of the "monk-calf of Fryberg" and the "pope-donkey of Rome", both anonymous (Alexandre, 1892), as we can imagine.

## WHAT'S SO FUNNY?

It is obviously easier to compare humans to animals than humans to objects. Therefore, the more the forms associated for a comical effect are distant in nature, the more intense is the transgression. Consequently, objectification is a technique that is extremely difficult to use and deserves to be emphasized. The engraver Desprez had the talent to marry object forms and animal ones, inspired by the rollicking texts of Rabelais.

I. François Desprez, Figure taken from *Les songes drôlatiques de Pantagruel* (Funny Dreams of Pantagruel, 1565), written by Rabelais

In a very jubilant tone, this 1565 illustrated reissue of Rabelais's work draws us into a cascade of emotions ranging from a smile to a burst of laughter, including astonishment at the fantastic engravings of François Desprez (circa 1530-1587). Desprez' creatures, such as this gingerly stepping barrel-tap, are deliriously anthropomorphic, anticipating surrealism, like the irreal visions of Hieronymus Bosch (1450-1516). Notice the drop that is running from the siphon nose, and the mouth in the form of a metallic handle, adding a sensitive touch to this half-human, half-machine creature.

François Rabelais, *Quart Livre*, 1552, Tome II, p.102

"Quaresmeprenant has for internal parts [...] kidneys like a trowel; the lower back like a padlock; the ureters pores like a cogwheel; the emulsifying veins like two small blowpipes; the spermatic vessels like a puff cake; the prostate like an inkpot; the bladder like a small crossbow; the neck of it like a bell clapper".

In Chapters 29 and 30, Pantagruel is attacked upon his arrival on the island of Tohu-Bohu (Jumble-Hubbub) because he is confused by the Andouille (Sausage-Head) with their enemy Quaresmeprenant (Lenten-Mistaking), described with a saraband of crazy comparisons for pages and pages, objectifying all parts of his body. Reading Rabelais' compendium triggers an intense burst of laughter, and in the same breath, offers us beautifully written and very harmonious texts. In fact, Rabelais uses a panoply of processes, exaggeration, objectification, punning, allegory, in the five volumes of his bawdy yet intellectually rigorous satire of his society.

Moreover, the complete work proceeds from a rather particular and unusual anthropomorphism because it operates a transfer from human to human. Pantagruel, his father Gargantua, his grandmother, Gargamelle, are giants, and along with his friend Panurge, represent beings larger than life. They live among others who swarm like dwarfs in their eyes. Bakhtine (1968) speaks about the carnivalesque laughter caused by the subversive inventions of Rabelais, that popular laughter redolent of medieval festivals. The illustrations by Desprez, then by Gustave Doré in the 19th-century edition, clearly reflect this disproportion between characters. Is this an indirect allusion to the way Rabelais, erudite writer, monk then physician, an extraordinary character and a true living encyclopedia, perceived himself among his fellows? His work deemed heretical by the Church, he was nevertheless tolerated, thanks to his multiple talents, and his satires have enjoyed fabulous success from their release to the present day.

With the birth of the printing press in the middle of the 15th century, the proliferation of images and texts such as *The Bible* led to the spread of new Lutheran ideas and the often-sanguinary quarrels that followed.

II. Anonymous, *Luther, Devil's Bagpipe*, mid-16th century.

## WHAT'S SO FUNNY?

One of the effects of the invention of the printing was to provoke a flood of images of all kinds. It is easy to understand why the authors of these first provocative pamphlets preferred to remain anonymous. Luther's physiognomy is shown here as a bagpipe; the nose stretches out like a pipe and the neck swells with air: he actually becomes the instrument of the devil. The elaboration of images halfway between medieval symbolic language and metaphorical new-wave games announces the birth of caricature.

In the 17th century, engravers rediscovered the "physiognomonia" of the Ancients. Back in Antiquity, thinkers such as Hippocrates and Galen (see Chapter 1) built a veritable charter of physiognomies in which they claimed to be able to identify the various human character types by "reading" their physiognomy. Studying the links between the faces of humans and animals, they found astonishing equivalences that would inspire generations of cartoonists. Many works treating "Physiognomonia" continued to appear during the following centuries. But it is the work of the Swiss pastor Lavater (1741–1801) which had the most profound impact on the perception of the links between human and animal forms for artists of his generation.

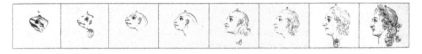

III. Lavater, *Physiognomic Fragments*, Extract, 1775–1778.

Lavater's *Physiognomonic Fragments for the Advancement of Human Knowledge and Love (Fragments physiognonomiques pour le progrès de la connaissance et de l'amour humains)* is a beauty to behold. Here, the artist progresses from the frog to Apollo in a metamorphosis spun by surprising threads: Lavater wanted to show that "what happens in the soul is expressed in the face [...] the more the inner passion becomes ugly, the more the beauty of the facial features fades". His work is a gold mine for artists, a genuine lexicon of animal/human associations.

Changing levels, let us pass rapidly from image games to the beginning of political caricature. The anecdote of Philipon's pear best demonstrates the force of the process of anthropomorphism and its power of transgression, to the point of becoming the preferred language of cartoonists.

IV. Honoré Daumier and Charles Philipon,
*Les poires*, (The Pears), *Le Charivari*, 1831.

Charles Philipon (1800-1862) is a French lithographer and journalist who founded and directed, in Paris, three of the world's first satirical periodicals, *La silhouette* (1829), *La Caricature* (1830) and *Le Charivari* (1832). The latter two were weeklies containing satirical texts and drawings, which would influence the creation of similar periodicals in other countries. The *Charivari* stood openly against policies of the sovereign Louis - Philippe's, the "citizen king" who did not meet the expectations of the people. During a trial provoked by the artist's repeated attacks on the king's power, Philipon engaged in a court demonstration on November 14, 1831, that went down in the annals of the history of caricature as a founding moment. He decided to defend himself with sketches of a royal portrait turning step by step into a pear, to show that the king can be represented by anything. Shortly after his trial, Philipon entrusted his sketches to Honoré Daumier (1808-1879), renowned artist and cartoonist by his side from the start, to engrave them. Daumier added a fourth drawing to Philipon's three original cartoons, and the sequence's success was phenomenal.

The walls of Paris began to be covered with pears. Then, the pears proliferated on walls everywhere in France. It was delirium. All contemporary cartoonists were doing it. Daumier designed *Une énorme poire pendue par les hommes du peuple* (A huge pear hanged by commoners), Grandville, *La naissance du juste milieu* (The birth of the middle way), Traviès, *Monsieur Mahieux, poiricide* (Mister Maheux pear murderer), Bouquet, *La poire et les pépins* (The pear and its seeds). Philipon himself, elated, kept on going with the publication of *Projet du monument expia-poire à élever sur la place*

## WHAT'S SO FUNNY?

*de la Révolution, précisément à la place où fut guillotiné Louis XVI* (Project of the expiapear monument to be erected on the Place de la Révolution, precisely on the spot where Louis XVI was guillotined) (*La caricature*, June 7, 1832). That was too much. Philipon served six months in prison and paid a fine. But he did not remain silent and continued throughout his career making fun of politics and politicos in his various satirical publications.

Across the satirical press, cartoonists loved to ridicule high-ranking persons by turning them into animals or objects. Then, progressively, images with movement, real or symbolised, took over, vividly incorporating this form of expression. **Animated cartoons** ran on anthropomorphism and then **comic art** used the same motif.

So, what happens in the mind of the spectator or reader when faced with a figure transformed by this process for a comic purpose? The first reaction is quick, caused by the instantaneity of the process: immediately one catches a subtlety that would otherwise take longer to establish; this individual is a rat, another is a frog and a third is a sow. As reader or listener, you understand the symbolic equivalences because you share the artist's culture. Someone without the same values, religious or political, could be horrified, scandalized to the point of pillorying the satirist. All the more, if in your culture, images are sacred or worse, forbidden, then you could cry blasphemy. In the latter context, authoritarian or downright dictatorial states have always sought to stifle such humour with all kinds of punishment going as far as the death sentence.

The second reaction to anthropomorphism, when countenanced, is fun. It's a playful process, dating back to childhood, inviting you to let your guard down and just let yourself be rocked. Anthropomorphism has an innocuous, fetching exterior. It traps you because, since you are defenseless and abandoning yourself, it can lead you to shadowy lands, where any critical mind is momentarily disconnected. A bit like an unreal journey, thought associations are sparked that you would not have consciously formulated. You smile and absorb the discourse.

Finally, because of these first two reasons, this process can tell you things that you would otherwise refuse. It opens your eyes to anomalies, to dysfunctions, to mistakes leaders make, to errors in society, to the cruelty we manifest without always realizing it. The laughter provoked by such a gag can also trigger a sudden understanding like a flash!

So, after caricatures, anthropomorphism expanded in the new art of comics and another pinnacle was attained with the transfer of human behavior to animals.

V. George Herriman, *"Krazy Kat"*, *New York Evening Journal*, circa 1913. All rights reserved.

The American Creole George Herriman (1880-1944) had the brilliant idea of humanizing animals in *Krazy Kat* (1913-1944), one of the first successful animal comics. Krazy Kat is of indeterminate gender, speaks a vague language, a mix of English, Yiddish and other tongues, moves in a constantly changing setting, and lives with two friends during the thirty years of its paper existence. The canvas is almost immutable: Krazy Kat has only one goal in life: save itself from Ignatz Mouse whose only goal in life is to lob bricks at Kat's head, in a funny inversion where the mouse chases the cat. There is another reversal: in love with the mouse, the cat believes throwing bricks is a proof of love. Finally, Dog Sergeant Pupp keeps stopping the mouse. In short, this absurd ballet serves as pretext for linguistic and visual discoveries close to the fantastic, but with a very simple design; all of which made this avant-garde comic strip a major work. The story represents a fine example of transposition of misunderstandings among different cultural groups. Undoubtedly, Herriman's critique goes well beyond interpersonal clashes and it is easy to see therein a broader satire of absurd conflicts, whether religious, social or cultural. No wonder it inspired a host of great artists: Chaplin, Picasso, Gertrude Stein, and even the Dadaists. Shows, cartoons and numerous books were spawned from public appreciation of *Krazy Kat* as one of the masterpieces of 20th-century comics. In fact, *Krazy Cat* is considered as the first on its list of the greatest comics of the 20th century by *The Comics Journal*.

## WHAT'S SO FUNNY?

VI. Sullivan, *Felix Trumps the Ace*,
(animated by Raoul Barré), 1926. All rights reserved.

Another great creation to humanize animals was initially a cartoon, *Felix the Cat*, launched in 1919 by Pat Sullivan (1888–1933) and Otto Messmer (1892–1983) with Raoul Barré (1874–1932). The cartoon *Felix the Cat* became a comic strip for the King Features Syndicate from 1923 until 1967. *Felix* continued its rise in comic books from 1948 and then on television from 1959. This work with modernist lines and strong flat areas of black and white takes another step forward in comic art symbolism by using poetically imaginative visual effects and numerous ideograms: Felix's tail turns into various tools depending on the stories; it can even grasp for a question mark above its head. By changing the narrative level, Felix plays on shapes but also on concepts, objectifying parts of its body like the tail or personalizing typographical elements. In his own way, Sullivan continues building on the invention of a graphic vocabulary by Lavater and Töpffer in the 19th century.

It can be noted that these two early creations using humanized animals were both also extremely innovative in humorous and symbolic language. And enjoyed remarkable success!

VII. Walt Disney (1901–1966), Mickey in *Steamboat Willie*, 1928.

A third player, Walt Disney, designed a gentle little mouse, Mickey Mouse, who initially appeared in *Steamboat Willie*, in 1928, the first cartoon with sound, used brilliantly. Indeed, the soundtrack of this medium-length film is a pure sound masterpiece. The visceral link between the gestures of animated creatures and the orchestral music is powerful and contributes to the comedy generated by the mechanics of the whole movie.

In *Steamboat Willie*, we have links between anthropomorphism and mechanization in a whirr of amazing movements. In fact, Disney was going to blur the lines somewhat in the talking animal world. While symbolic language was powerful in early animal comics, Disney rather watered down its own, leaving no critical essence in order to make them merely charming.

So, Disney quickly left the territory of experimentation and chose to transpose the "American way of life" to the animal world. In fact, Disney imagined an animal world that constitutes the perfect counterexample of the process of symbolic anthropomorphism. He added talking animals to his menagerie, Donald Duck and the dogs Goofy and Pluto; then he included female friends, nephews, houses. Soon afterwards, he had these cartoons translated and distributed throughout the world. Their global success was rapid and nothing could stop him: toys, clothes, hats, all reflected the investment in total merchandising. Disney launched paper comics in 1932. Then, he turned to the production of animated feature films reproducing children's stories. For their part, after a promising start, his animal heroes were aimed resolutely at children to their great delight, but the characters lost their symbolic force and wound up becoming only cute. They just represented themselves and no longer evoked the qualities or faults associated with reference animals. Eventually, Disney animals mutated into animal transpositions of conventional human behaviors. They're mice, ducks, dogs, but they could be rattlesnakes, dinosaurs or groundhogs! They are nothing more than little humans who would have been disguised as a mouse or a dog for a Halloween masquerade!

In everyday life, there is a tendency to endow objects with human components, in a way so spontaneous that these terms have become commonplace, such as the foot of a chair or the head of a bed. In contemporary comics, the human-object transfer stands as a powerful figure in underground territory. But this mode of thinking can also evoke hallucinogenic visions and actions, whose subversive subtext can read as a rejection of conventional life and a critique of the society at large.

# WHAT'S SO FUNNY?

VIII. Julie Doucet, "What an Intense City", *Dirty Plotte*, 1988, 2019.

In her major opus, the bilingual *Dirty Plotte*, Doucet builds a quite new language where objects become alive. They move, talk and react to the action, which could be interpreted in different ways. Firstly, what comes to mind is a critique of the many mechanized aspects of life in the Big City, New York in fact. And as a result, it seems here that human beings are dehumanized, emptied of their emotions, so, secondly, "Julie" might feel objects are more alive than humans in the intense City.

In this object-human anthropomorphism, the objects talk and move like people. The fire hydrant is the one most sympathetic towards Julie, so to speak. Another type of object has an important role in these comix: beer cans, walking around Julie's feet like little animals, and reacting to what is happening. Here, a beer can even tells the fire hydrant to open the letter ("Open it!") held in its hand. Altruistic, they take care of each other, unlike humans who seem quite indifferent. Furthermore, the indifference rubs off on her, and in an inversion of emotions, she is looking at her luggage instead of being concerned with the poor man just being hit by a car behind her. Are big cities dehumanizing people? Doucet seems to ask.

Anthropomorphism can give surprising results.

IX. Janet Perlmann, *Bully Dance*, ©NFB, 2000.

In this work of Janet Perlmann (1954- ), a Canadian animator who has been working at the National Film Board of Canada since 1972, the game of transfers plays on multiple levels of humour. Perlmann creates a denunciation of bullying in an allegory wherein creatures with ambiguous contours, a mix of ants and dwarf hippos, move in a mechanical ballet. She knows certain messages get through more easily if they are not said head-on: the humorous transfer hides the harshness of the phenomenon under an amusing exterior. Thus, rendered defenseless, intimidators, often the young people to whom these short films are addressed, are more likely to understand the pain they are causing.

## Mechanization of movement

In the mid-19th century, with the emergence of photography, artists could get in touch with all segments of a given movement and they began to play with lines to unlock the secrets of bodily motion. At that time, main codes were born and would serve both cartoonists and animation filmmakers during the next century. One dissects the mystery of trajectories; another synthesizes their mechanisms. "Motion lines" belong to this new vocabulary. Horizontal, vertical and concentric lines intersect in the images to signify the course of gestures in space.

## WHAT'S SO FUNNY?

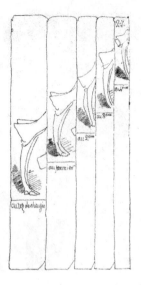

X. Rodolphe Töpffer, *The Story of Albert*, 1845.

Rodolphe Töpffer here literally slices Albert's back and replicates him several times to show the different stages of a progression. Now and then, space-time is indicated as if it were an inert matter that could be cut with a knife. Thus, he carves bodies in the air; while these body slices expose nothing bloody, they, on the contrary and in an astonishing way, make people laugh by the mechanics of the process.

XI. Caran d'Ache, *Deux scènes de duel* (Two Scenes of a Duel) circa 1890.

Caran d'Ache (pseud. Emmanuel Poiré, 1858-1909), was a French cartoonist who participated in the graphic innovations that would give birth to comics. Here, he serves us undisguised slices of the fallen protagonist from that cruel tradition of duels. In doing so, he gives us the impression of hearing the weapon whistle as it slices through the space densified by his pen. And yet, far from being repulsive, the scene, in fact, makes people laugh by its detached, "objectual" side. We are surely faced with this mysterious phenomenon that Bergson called "a momentary anesthesia of the heart", whereby transforming the human into an object (here, the atrocity of cutting the human body into slices) allows us to create a distance from our emotions. And laughter bursts forth instead of the reflex of horror.

This propensity to replicate objects in space will continue to delight readers even in modern comics as a code now understood by all, where the human body almost becomes a machine, or in any case, disembodied. Piece by piece, we see the humorous visual language elaborating the universe of a strong critique of the modern world and its indifference to individual needs.

As we have seen, the origin of slapstick, or volley of punches for comic purposes, is undoubtedly as old as the world itself. In popular theater, in *Commedia dell'arte*, in all the antics of clowns and other public comedians, we often witness these delirious scenes in which the performers start to hit each other without causing apparent pain, because of a simple desire to let off steam, much to the public's amusement.

The underground discourse coming from the 1960s and 1970s and the mainstream adult comics that broke the codes during the 1980s reflected great satisfaction in opening the floodgates. The multiplicity of hands and feet, the many lines streaking the space in a box, all these signs mark excitement at its peak, whatever the cause, happy or not.

Gesture replication, but in a different direction, more colored by apparent insensibility, also exists in basic manga language. Mangakas like to repeat the hands, faces or mimicry of their characters as if they were reflected in corridors of mirrors, indicating simultaneously excessive movement, trepidation of the action and hysteria of almost disembodied protagonists. With manga trending around the globe since the 1990s, the youngest artists are having a blast with numerous, totally unrealistic battle scenes wherein bodies no longer seem to suffer, hence reproducing the same effect as painless blows with sticks in the infancy of silent cinema. Here, successions of explosive squares place heroines and heroes in various positions either flying or still more unreal, floating in the air. Flying machines, fighting machines, bodies no longer seem to contain blood or emotions; only well-

## WHAT'S SO FUNNY?

established mechanisms animate them. Without passing judgment on the insensitivity these narratives may involve, let us point out that many debates have taken place and are ongoing about the long-term effects on young audiences of watching these mechanical battles over and over again in youth comics and video games.

Let us leave the conclusion to Bergson since he deepened the reflection on the irresistible comical effect of "mechanics plastered on the living". "This vision of the mechanical and the living being inserted into each other guides us obliquely towards the vaguer image of any stiffness applied to the mobility of life (Bergson, 1901)."

# CHAPTER 9
# WORD AND IMAGE GAMES

## The Pun

To pun is playing one word instead of another because of their similarity in sound.

Why, upon hearing sound games with homophones, do some people roll on the floor with laughter while others remain unmoved, or even find the exercise completely stupid? The mystery of humour deploys its full meaning here. The pun is arguably the most popular word game. It is often said that the spoken word and the referred word "sound the same". We understand that this word game is first and foremost funny verbally; we could say "auditorily". If we read it instead of hearing it, we will have to "say it in our head" to really understand its essence. There are so many homophones in every language that it is a joy for stand-up comedians to play with sounds in this way. Another distinction of the pun: it is untranslatable, obviously, and this source of amusement for those who share the same linguistic if not cultural affiliation plays into the bonding it implies.

Shakespeare, *The Second Part of King Henry IV* (1600), Act 2, scene IV.

PISTOL: God save you, Sir John!

FALSTAFF: Welcome, Ancient Pistol. Here, Pistol, I charge you with a cup of sack. Do you discharge upon mine hostess.

## WHAT'S SO FUNNY?

PISTOL: I will discharge upon her, Sir John, with two bullets.

FALSTAFF: She is pistol-proof, sir; you shall not hardly offend her.

HOSTESS: Come, I'll drink no proofs nor no bullets. I'll drink no more than will do me good, for no man's pleasure, I.

PISTOL: Then to you, Mistress Dorothy; I will charge you.

DOLL: Charge me? I scorn you, scurvy companion. What, you poor, base, rascally, cheating, lack-linen mate? Away, you moldy rogue, away! I am meat for your master.

FALSTAFF: No more, Pistol, I would not have you go off here.

Discharge yourself of our company, Pistol.

In this comical interlude between a buffoonish gentleman Falstaff and Pistol, his ensign, we find a vivid example of Shakespeare's fondness for puns. The wordplay turns on the likeness between military equipment/functions and sexual performance so the comedy is both verbal, in characters' names and action verbs for instance, and psychological in rather a proto-Freudian way. It should be added about bawdy jokes that there is always a double movement in the mind of the person who laughs at them. The ambivalence of the feeling adds to the enjoyment of this type of comedy: both shame at laughing at vulgarities and delight that the joke glides under the radar of proprieties precisely, because of the varnish of the first-degree text, the laugher has the luxury of not feeling guilty.

In everyday life, some people have a real gift for finding the most delectable puns. You can play with just one syllable or with a set of syllables which will then create a delightful polysemic pattern. The enjoyment in discovering a sound game is an intrinsic part of triggering laughter. Indeed, all combinations of verbal trickery elicit amusement, to varying degrees. Many stand-up comedians have made this their foolproof recipe.

Nowadays, the new generation has a wide range of fun at their fingertips: not only do social networks feed them endlessly with the best finds from YouTube or comic sites, but social networks now allow everyone to become the stars in their own creations, whatever their age. Indeed, we even see children, sometimes quite young, obviously encouraged by their parents, producing comic scenes, some of which quickly go viral. The line is becoming blurred between the frankly comical scenes, just for fun, we could say, and those which turn into money-makers. Sometimes, their creators' popularity can even lead companies to pay them to become influencers. On the one hand, then, this new version of amateur theater; on the other, comedy sites, often run by professionals. Now, anybody can drink instantly, with a click, at the fountain of multiple websites dedicated to humour with all kinds of word games, on and on.

## Other Word Games

No doubt fairground antics and long family evenings since time immemorial have been the crucible for all kinds of word games. From the marketplace acrobat of Antiquity to the comedian on the contemporary stage, artists of the comic word have juggled the most diverse puns, mixing and matching them. Recently, a researcher, Silvia Ferrara, an Italian philologist, made an astonishing discovery in this regard. Professor at the University of Bologna and director of the Inscribe program (Invention of Scripts and their Beginnings), she claimed that the birth of letters, the basis of all writing, comes from our taste for puns and rebuses. She has found evidence in ancient sites that it is from this mechanism that humans gave birth to writing: the transcription of puns.

The pun synthesizes a number of word games. But there are many other kinds of word play out there, of which here are a few examples. The **spoonerism** is an inversion, either intentional or inadvertent, of syllables in a group of words whose end result is often an obscene sentence. It is a transposition of sounds, often the initial consonants, in two or more words, such as "a shoving leopard" in place of "loving shepherd". The term *spoonerism* is derived from the name of William A. Spooner (1844–1930), who had a reputation for making these slips of the tongue. Spoonerisms are fairly common in everyday speech and were well known, of course, even before Reverend Spooner lent his name to the phenomenon.

**Phonetic language** is a group of words concentrated into a few letters reproducing their sound but not their spelling, varying from nation to nation. **Linguistic particularisms** make people laugh as much with "a wink and a nudge"- hey, hey, the others do not understand -, as by their flavorful hues. One can mix accent, particularisms and puns. Grassroots dialects provide inexhaustible comic sources. Regionalisms can provide a source of hilarity and their use is fre-

## WHAT'S SO FUNNY?

quent in comedy monologues and humorous scenarios. Orally funny, word-play combinations can also be extremely comical when written, whether in playbooks, film scripts, or printed monologues.

Here are some examples attributed to Robert Chamberlain (1607–1660), *Conceits, Clinches, Flashes, and Whimzies* (1639):

- "One being asked what Countryman he was, he answered, a Middlesex man. The other told him, being he was neither of the male sex nor of the female sex but of a middlesex, he must then be a Hermaphrodite.
- A Smith, said one, is the most pragmatical fellow under the Sun, for he hath always many irons in the fire.
- One asked what the reason was that few women loved to eat eggs. It was answered, because they cannot endure to bear the yoke."

Finally, word jokes generated by chance or ignorance can be used in the context of compilations of funny stories, for example. Indeed, gems found in student writing, confusions of sound or meanings, dutifully transcribed by teachers with a lively sense of humour, can serve as basic material for comic collections, to the point that, real or made-up, the gems elicit spontaneous laughter. Children's words, which some parents collect religiously, are often puns spontaneously created by toddlers learning to speak. If we could decode what toddlers first understand when they confuse phonemes when learning language, we would undoubtedly split our sides with laughter. French psychoanalyst Françoise Dolto recounts some particularly amusing misconceptions that child patients told her in *La cause des enfants* (1985). A very funny derivative of these word jokes due to chance is that particular habit of coming up with real family names whose sense evokes the profession of their owner.

As we saw in Chapter 4, the nature of **onomatopoeia** places it between word and image games when seen in comics and cartoons. Onomatopoeia is a sequence of letters that imitates a natural sound, like "buzz", "hiss", or "thud", evoking a bee, snake or angry cat, a heavy object dropped on a floor, respectively. A host of words obey this rule. Given their comic charge, onomatopoeias can turn up, in any evocative text, but above all, they shine brightly in comics, where they are found floating between the balloons containing the words, as if they filled this symbolic space like sound effects in the movies or in cartoons. They are shaped according to movement, and the size of the letters varies according to the intensity of the sound; they can be projected at full speed into space. The letters of onomatopoeia crushed, torn apart under the impact of an explosion, for example, are transformed into objects: they change reality to shift from the signifier (the letter) to the signified (the explosion). A formidable sound game, onomatopoeia sometimes winds up, in extreme comics, becoming an actress in her own right, to the point of suffocating human protagonists.

## Double Meaning

When our brains go back and forth in a joyous mix of interpretation, we often talk about double meaning or equivocation. In both senses, our understanding continually oscillates between the two meanings, hence the name.

We said at the outset that puns and word play are there to make people laugh; you could even say, a bit of a silly laugh. Punning sprinkles the routines of comedians on stage, as well as the lyrics of comic song booklets, and the texts of comics and cartoons. It gives rhythm, opens the door for another, deeper level of discourse.

The double meaning of a given situation has a name from the commedia dell'arte: the *quiproquo*, which in this context means "misunderstanding." Such misunderstanding is the basis of the comedy of situations that has animated popular theater since the dawn of time, then, eventually, comic cinema. Disguises, wigs, and makeup are intrinsic parts of this game within the game. The funniest thing about this type of misunderstanding is the bond between the viewer or reader and the author of the work. Usually, it is almost immediately apparent that this is an attempt at deception, and the question which arises is: when will the dupe understand what is happening or will the dupe ever understand? The process is similar in its intention to the

## WHAT'S SO FUNNY?

aside: to turn spectators into accomplices and thus to increase their pleasure tenfold.

Thus, in the double meaning, there can be equivocation either about the identity of a character, or about the meaning of words, or, finally, about the whole meaning of an action which can lead to two interpretations. With the mask, one camouflages the face, thus the real identity of the actor. With the double meaning, the masquerade is twofold. Onto the theatrical or cinematographic convention which enables the spectator to know that the character is an actor, we superimpose a second masquerade: this actor is also playing a character playing a character!

> Molière, *Le malade imaginaire* (The Imaginary Invalid) (1673), Act 3, scene X.

TOINETTE (disguised as a doctor): I see, sir, that you are staring at me. How old do you think I am?

ARGAN: I believe that at most you can be twenty-six or twenty-seven years old.

TOINETTE: Ah! Ah! Ah! Ah! Ah! I am ninety.

ARGAN: Ninety!

TOINETTE: Yes, you see the effects of the secrets of my art, in keeping me so fresh and vigorous.

ARGAN: By my faith, here is a handsome young old man for ninety years!

TOINETTE: [...] I can see that you don't know me yet. Who is your doctor?

ARGAN: Dr. Purgon.

TOINETTE: This man is not written up on my shelves among the great doctors. What does he say you're sick with?

ARGAN: He says it's my liver and others say it's my spleen.

TOINETTE: They are all ignorant. It's the lungs that you're sick with.

ARGAN: The lungs?

> Molière's mockery is obviously directed against doctors, who, according to him, are saying and prescribing anything. The irony is patent in this Toinette-doctor who says the opposite of what others say just to show the folly of it all. The misunderstanding in this scene is based on disguise: a change in sex, age and social status all at the same time. Toinette continues the ridiculous dialogue wherein she prescribes for the hypochondriac a diet of feasting, and then suggests that he cut off his arm and put out his eye ... In short, the deception taking place throughout the scene gives the greatest pleasure to the spectators, who enjoy their connivance with the one carrying out the deception.

As Molière shows us here, most of the time the public is complicit in the imposture. But then, why is it so funny if we know the true nature of the travesty? Because actually, it's the whole scheme that's funny. We have fun with the deception. We can go from one side to the other, imagining ourselves sometimes on the dupe's side, sometimes on the manipulator's one. How does the one being duped manage not to notice the deception? Sometimes, however, the public does not know that deception is occurring; they will learn it at the same time as the dupe. Finally, we can also see a misunderstanding due to a shared misconception between characters, either because of a resemblance, two identical twins for example, or a lack of knowledge, or perhaps a chance meeting.

> Conan Doyle, "How it Happened, Tales of Twilight",
> *Strand Magazine*, September 1913.

(*He had an accident in a car*) 'I was quite unable to move. Indeed, I had not any desire to move. But my senses were exceedingly alert. I saw the wreck of the motor lit up by the moving lanterns. I saw the little group of people and heard the hushed voices. There were the lodge-keeper and his wife, and one or two more. They were taking no notice of me, but were very busy round the car. Then suddenly, I heard a cry of pain.

"The weight is on him. Lift it easy", cried a voice.

"It's only my leg!", said another one, which I recognised as Perkins's. "Where's the master?" he cried.

"Here I am," I answered, but they did not seem to hear me. They were all bending over something which lay in front of the car.

Stanley laid his hand upon my shoulder, and his touch was inexpressibly soothing. I felt light and happy, in spite of all.

# WHAT'S SO FUNNY?

"No pain, of course?" said he.

"None", said I.

"There never is," said he.

And suddenly a wave of amazement passed over me. Stanley! Stanley! Why, Stanley had surely died of enteric at Bloemfontein in the Boer War!

"Stanley!" I cried, and the words seemed to choke my throat – "Stanley, you are dead."

He looked at me with the same old gentle, wistful smile.

"So are you," he answered.'

> The skill of the great British writer Conan Doyle (1859–1930) is evident in both the judiciously chosen context and in the small clues with which he sprinkles his text ("No pain", "of course", "There never is"). This accentuates our doubt until the final punch, a marvel of repartee, in this end of scene which is anything but macabre. There are still hints of doubt in our mind, the narration resembling so strangely that of a dream wherein the sensations seem frozen that we cannot help thinking it is a dream and not the words of a dead man!

In the equivocation about the overall meaning of an action, our mind as reader or spectator is constantly moving, hesitating over the decoding necessary to understand the scene.

## The Visual Pun

Just as the process of anthropomorphism is particularly suited to visual humour, the pun is, by its very nature, verbal. But there is also the **visual pun**, and it is among the sophisticated comic processes requiring boldness to use. The major difference between the process of anthropomorphism and the visual pun is that the visual pun combines two forms of objects while human forms are involved in anthropomorphism. The pun in images associates two forms whose profile is similar but which are often very far apart by nature. The pun has fun with forms as it does with words. The analogous transfer between the shape of words or numbers and any logo or symbol is widely used in cartooning and in comic advertising.

# MIRA FALARDEAU

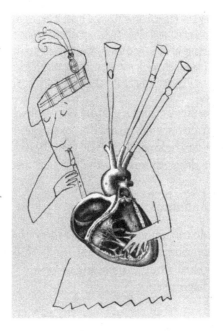

I. Tony Ungerer, "The Bagpiper", *Weltshonerz*, 1961. All rights reserved.

When Alsatian cartoonist Ungerer (1931-2019) turns the bagpipe into a heart, he is playing with similarity of shapes. Does he mean to tell us that the musician is playing with all his heart? Or that his instrument is a part of himself? The visual pun has a poetic tinge. It brings us into another land, where words and forms yield other senses, floating between two worlds, the real one and the one of dreams. Ungerer, a poet of drawing, has the rare honor of having a museum totally dedicated to him in Strasbourg, the Tomi Ungerer Museum.

II. Chaval, "The Sax Player", circa 1950. All rights reserved.

## WHAT'S SO FUNNY?

In the same way, when the French artist Chaval (pseud. Yvan Le Louarn) (1915-1968) sits an old gentleman in his chair and places a saxophone exhaling smoke in his hands, one would think he is smoking his sax. And our eyes alternately go from the depicted sax to the simulated cigar. Chaval shows a melancholy humour, his beings wander through a dehumanized world; he thus underlines the stupidity of the society which is his.

We often see cartoonists using a graphic symbol whose shape evokes another object, strictly visual puns. For example, when Pat Sullivan changes the tail of his beloved Felix the Cat (1919–1997) into a question mark, well, he does not give us the answer, just the question...

### Visual Double Meaning

In the visual double meaning, our eyes do the same, they move from one direction to the other in a back-and-forth of understanding. For that reason, the visual double meaning is one of the favorite processes of critical discourse.

III. Ares, (The Proliferation of Arms), 2012. All rights reserved.

Ares (Aristides Esteban Hernandez Guerrero) (1963-), a Cuban editorial cartoonist, seamlessly develops a visual language often unaccompanied by words, very effective in overcoming language barriers. The power of his messages is thereby accentuated. The double meaning is doubled here by a metonymy, which shows a part for the whole, here handguns for warfare. The skyscrapers of the American megalopolis seem to rise out of the barrels of American firepower. That is the cri de coeur from the Cuban opponent of the hated regime which subjects his island-nation to its whims, such as the embargo, the ongoing occupation of Guantanamo, obstacles to obtaining money transfers and visas, and *tutti quanti*. The sobriety of the message does not hide its violence, but rather increases it tenfold.

I repeat here the difference between the visual pun and the visual double meaning: the first has no sense, and is a game, while the second has one and often two senses, strong and powerful.

IV. Louison, "L'eau", (Water), 2012.

Louison (pseud. Louise Angelergues) (1985-) is a French cartoonist from the Web generation. She is often featured on the *L'OBS* (former *Nouvel Observateur*) website, and has her own blog, which is a common springboard nowadays. Her language is always clear, she does not encumber herself with settings, goes straight to the point and often uses drawings likewise without words, in a search for purity of discourse. If I understand that the figure is drinking the earth, depleting its reserves of water, it is because in fact, I mainly see in his hands a kind of collapsible gourd emptying as he drinks. But then I come back down to earth, and the message has sunk in.

Unlike the visual pun, a game of lines, visual double meaning is a shifting between forms logically bound together, most of the time connected by a necessary, metonymic relation. Alternating the two senses, it leads us to question ourselves.

# CHAPTER 10
# NONSENSE AND SNAPSHOT

**N**onsense consists of a text, gesture, form or action devoid of meaning or contrary to reality or to logic, hence absurd.

If the notion of "absurd" is evoked in Cicero's *De Oratore* (55 BCE) as part of his discourse explaining rhetoric, it is in 19th-century England that the word "nonsense" gained currency and became with "absurd" a form of art expression.

I. John Tenniel, *Alice's Adventures in Wonderland,* by Lewis Carroll (pseud. of Charles Dodgson), 1865.

## MIRA FALARDEAU

"Alice asked the Cheshire Cat, who was sitting in a tree, 'What road do I take?'

The cat asked, 'Where do you want to go?'

'I don't know,' Alice answered.

'Then,' said the cat, 'it really doesn't matter, does it?'"

Initially, the English writer Lewis Carroll (1832–1898), also a mathematician and scientist, did not write for children. On the advice of his editor, he slightly transformed his *Alice in Wonderland* to adapt it for children. Richly illustrated by John Tenniel's prints, *Alice* is a masterpiece of nonsense. When I first read it when I was 7 years old, I didn't at all perceive the story's illogical aspect. Nor did my pre-logical mind notice its highly comical side. And I was only hoping for one thing, to find the elixir and become as small as a mouse! I found it deliciously pleasant to be able to think of becoming tiny. It was only during subsequent readings that I grasped the totally crazy aspect of Carroll's universe, between the white rabbit for whom time flies too quickly and the mad hatter for whom time stands still, between a card game coming to life and an atrocious queen thirsty for beheadings. When at the very beginning of the story, Alice falls into the hollow tree, her descent is very long. If the text is read slowly, her fall can take more than two minutes: she has time to ask herself numerous questions: has she fed her cat correctly, what is she becoming, where is she going? Such a drop evokes the sensation of falling in a dream, the constant oscillation in our mind between reality and fantasy. In the same way, in front of an absurd comic composition, we are constantly tossed between logic and illogic. The immense talent of Carroll enables him to stun us in between these two worlds, with a logical illogicality! Even if we can no longer see it, *Alice in Wonderland* was for its contemporaries above all a biting satire of the Victorian model, conservative and gloomy, as well as an anthology of allusions to well-known people of that time. Anthropomorphism, political and cultural satire, puns, social metaphor, *Alice* offered a rainbow of comic forms, the nonsensical dimension being their quintessence.

A more poetic vein of nonsense produced the sensitive texts of Irish authors Oscar Wilde (1854–1900) with "*On the Importance of Being Constant*". Or Bernard Shaw (1856–1950), Nobel Prize of Literature in 1925, who used to say: "Animals are my friends. I don't eat my friends" (Quoted by Pearson, 1963) like the good vegetarian that he was.

Let us allow ourselves a parenthesis. In this current era of literature solely aimed at children, we miss those fictional works for audiences of all ages, where a child's first reading was subsequently enriched by reading the same story again and again, with the level of understanding following cognitive evolution. For instance, in *The Adventures of Tintin* by Hergé, adults could enjoy higher degrees of intellectual

# WHAT'S SO FUNNY?

amusement through the surrealist visions of Tintin drugged in *Cigars of the Pharaoh* (1955), while children might only see funny pictures. In these gradational readings by adults and children, we have a vivid illustration of the progressive perception of the absurd.

Of all figures, nonsense is both the easiest to detect and most complex to produce for humorous purposes. Indeed, it is not enough to imagine an impossible phenomenon for it to be funny! Considerable subtlety is required to wield the art of comic illogicality. As Freud so rightly observed about the need to superimpose processes in order to achieve humour: "Other processes still allow us to recover the nonsense and derive pleasure from it: the caricature, the hyperbole, the parody, cross-dressing, employ it and then achieve 'comic nonsense'" (Freud, 1905).

Afterwards, we find this same love of the absurd in Europe at the beginning of the 20th century with the birth of surrealism. With Dadaism or the dada movement, nonsensical speech came into vogue. One of the few artistic movements frankly and decidedly comical above all, this current of anarchic expression was born in Zurich in 1916 and spread throughout Europe. In 1919, it found a second momentum in Paris under the leadership of Tristan Tzara. All art forms were shaken up by this iconoclastic art laughing at everything, literature, plastic arts, cinema, dance, photography, music, as well as at itself.

The unusual works of the artist Marcel Duchamp (1887–1968) constitute in themselves a whole program, such as his notorious urinal incarnated as a work of art (*Fontaine,* 1917) or his bottle of *Belle Haleine (Beautiful Breath)* perfume (a "ready-made", 1921) with *Rrose Sélavy (Éros c'est la vie)* (Eros is Life, 1920) printed on it. The theory then affirmed with obvious cynicism: you just have to decide that an object is a work of art for it to become one! Incidentally, Duchamp had started his career as a cartoonist and had, among other things, participated in the *Salon des Humoristes* of 1907 at the Palais des Glaces in Paris. Cartoonists were called "humorists" in those days. By ridiculing all established codes, the dada movement had a major influence in the modern world and on much of 20th-century art. This derisive burst of laughter was born after the disasters of the First World War. As its founder, Tristan Tzara (1896–1967), clearly explained 40 years later, in *"Lampisteries"* (Lamp Rooms) (1963): "Dada was not only absurd, not just a joke, dada was the expression of a very strong adolescent pain, born during the 1914 war. What we wanted was to wipe out current values, but precisely for the benefit of the highest

116

## MIRA FALARDEAU

human values." "Dada is a cry; it is the void erected as an art of the living "(Jean Arp).

Artists then became fascinated by free association of words or automatic writing that ultimately produces totally nonsensical creations. Surrealist authors immersed themselves in a dreamlike state of mind where thoughts follow one another without apparent connection. A tangent of dada gave birth to surrealism and a tangent of surrealism became what André Breton (1896–1966), father of surrealism, called black humour.

> Jacques Prévert, *La tentative de description d'un dîner de têtes à Paris-France* (The Attempt to Describe a Dinner of Heads in Paris-France), quoted by André Breton in *Anthologie de l'humour noir* (*Anthology of Black Humor*) (1947)

"Those who piously ...
Those who copiously...
Those who inaugurate [...]
Those who stand the dead
Those who bayonet ... we (sic)
Those who give cannons to children
Those who give children to cannons [...]
Those whose giant wings prevent from flying
Those who put a wolf mask[1] on their faces when they eat
    mutton..."

For dozens of stanzas, Jacques Prévert (1900–1977), French poet, writer and screenwriter, intones anaphorically that haunting imagery. And he continues in an increasingly morbid mode with "mothers with dead heads" and "flies so bored, they die and fall from the ceiling" ... in a powerful chanting where cynical, light and sad stanzas envelop us in a hazy melancholy. The play *Dinner of Heads* premiered in Paris in 1951. We must not forget that we are amidst the aftermath of the catastrophic Second World War and that people's minds are still in shock. Here too, we are in the same movement of catharsis as inside Tzara's scream after the First World War.

Free association gave birth to a vast artistic current in poetry, plastic arts, cinema, to name only these languages; but the movement goes far beyond the theme of this study. This exercise of freedom

---

[1] A pun in French: a wolf is also a mask.

# WHAT'S SO FUNNY?

often results in surprising, overwhelming or insurgent compositions, wherein humour is not necessarily a significant motivation.

Later, with black humour, text and image serve as witness to life's absurdity through morbid or sadistic words albeit pronounced in a matter-of-fact way, as if stating the obvious. "You love your sister, well, take another piece!" is its style, and a whole school of illustrators and then cartoonists furthered this trend during the hippie movement of the 1960s and 1970s. That trend continues its spread on new platforms like Tik Tok.

Chas Addams, "The Addams family", *The New Yorker* (1938–1988)

That liberal American magazine published one of the first series of black humour, signed by the American cartoonist Charles Addams (1912–1988). In his cartoons, he wields this new form of humour, by generating an atypical family in total rejection of the American way of life. The two children, daughter Wednesday and son Pugsley, play macabre games: Wednesday cuts off the head of her Marie Antoinette doll or has fun electroshocking her brother. Living in a grim Gothic Revival-style mansion on top of a hill, all the creatures in this series are unreal: the servant is called the Hand and is, in fact, a hand that walks on its own! Paranormal phenomena, dark aesthetics prefiguring the neo-gothic fashion fad, nothing is spared to make readers shiver with delight; superimposing childhood and sadism would doubtless scandalize were not the cartoons spiced with such crazy humour. The recipe for a monster success is here! *The Addams Family* is actually very popular as well in movies as in animated series and video games, or in books, TV sitcoms, and even musical comedies.

Other prestigious names helped make *The New Yorker* a magazine at the forefront of absurd humour characteristic of the mid-20th century, an era profoundly wounded by World War II and its atrocities. Brilliant cartoonists distinguished themselves in the weekly, such as James Thurber (1894–1961) (*The Secret Life of Walter Mitty*, a book turned into a film in 2013, US, dir. Stiller), as gifted in his comical writing as in his caustic drawings, or Saul Steinberg (1914–1999), poet of the *ligne claire* (clear line), a stripped-down drawing style, as we saw in Chapter 3.

The humorous drawing, because of its instantaneity and its forcefulness, has been chosen as principal vehicle by the artists enamored of "black humour", typical of left-wing intellectuals in the United Kingdom, USA, and France, as well.

One of the significant constants of comically absurd texts is a kind of loop in logic that gives the reader the impression of going around in circles. As before, in *Alice in Wonderland*, we were wondering where this naughty Alice wanted to go, and even if she wanted to go anywhere at all or stay in the same place.

Director Woody Allen with *Mere Anarchy* (2007), a collection of eighteen short stories including ten pre-published in *The New Yorker*, reached new heights of nonsense. "I awoke Friday, and because the universe is expanding, it took longer than usual to find my robe." As in his movie dialogues, which are for the most part veritable little masterpieces of cynicism, he often tends to confront two worlds, one serious and the other innocuous.

We find the same movement in the Canadian writer Stephen Leacock (1969–1944) with *My Financial Career*.

II. Gerald Potterton, *My Financial Career*, ©NFB, 1962, based on a text by Stephen Leacock.

The film begins like this: "When I go into a bank, I get rattled. The clerks rattle me; the wickets rattle me; the sight of the money rattles me; everything rattles me. The moment I cross the threshold of a bank and attempt to transact business there, I become an irresponsible idiot."

> Unlike many comic writers who frequented other languages before putting their discoveries on paper, Stephen Leacock (1869-1944) came to writing almost by accident. Nothing predestined this political science professor at prestigious McGill University in Montreal to an international reputation, acquired through his humorous writings (Literary Lapses, Nonsense Novels, My Financial Career, Little Town), which assigned a significant role to the absurd and the incongruous. In the cartoon adaptation of his short story, a fellow who clearly suffers from extreme embarrassment, if not social

## WHAT'S SO FUNNY?

phobia, opens a bank account with $56, putting on airs of a very rich man, and then makes a withdrawal of the same amount before the stunned eyes of the bank employees. Yes, we understand this poor chap's anguish, but what's the purpose? The story is altogether tedious. He has made a deposit and then taken it out. And that is all. End of story. So what? But we laugh, simply, surprised by such futile gestures, no doubt reminiscent of the empty speeches some people give for hours on end, leading us to believe a fascinating story will follow. But no, nothing happens. The narrative is, remarkably, totally insignificant. This is a comic situation in front of nothing. But this "nothing" could be an allusion to the incredible carnival of banking and banks, and a gibe at the rich.

"Olga, you don't have to wear a mask—you're a potato."

III. Victoria Roberts, *"Olga, you don't have to wear a mask- you're a potato"*, *New Yorker*, April 4, 2021.

The American cartoonist Victoria Roberts (1957- ), author and performer, has spent a part of her life in Australia. Her work has regularly been published in *The New Yorker* since 1988, amid other collaborations. Notably, the artist knows how to blend an underlying message into an absurd language. The above nonsensical potatoes recall the biased discourses about the mask during the seemingly endless pandemic. We can see here that the comic impact would not have been so strong if Roberts had stood two rabbits or two beavers upright, speaking. The distance between reality and absurd invention has great importance in nonsense discourse.

Towards the end of the 20th century, nonsense would become so common as to be hardly noticeable, a mere trademark of expression for a certain rebellious school of thought, comprising artists and readers alike.

# MIRA FALARDEAU

## The Snapshot

A tangent of nonsense appears in moving images of humour, whether in cartoons, experimental cinema or, subsequently, in comics and humorous drawings: this is called the snapshot. A simplification of movement, as if in suspension, frozen in space and time, the snapshot is instantly comical. Obviously, the snapshot can only be visual, and borrows its name from photography.

*Road Runner,* as we have seen in Chapter 4, serves up an eloquent example when the bird finds itself in the void following a wild chase by the coyote: he is frozen in the dizzying immensity of an endless precipice, and he watches us spectators watching him, one foot in the air, petrified in the snapshot, seemingly telling us: "Like me, you think, don't you, that I'm going to crash in a few seconds?" Added to the delicious sensation of stopping time is the illusion of foreseeing the action. The illusion is fictitious, of course, since everything is already posed in the snapshot. This is somewhat like the "Deus ex Machina" in ancient Greek theater that permitted the gods to fly. The snapshot is especially fun in humorous drawings. It can also freeze a possible real movement, just to give us the added satisfaction of completing the movement mentally.

But with the repeated flights of superheroes and now superheroines, nonsense is receding to the extent that it is difficult to feel with the same force. Fluctuations in the space of heroes from current cooperative video games such as "Fortnite" (Epic Games, 2017-) are becoming almost normal with their 500 million players registered in 2023!

It can be noted that, unlike other techniques remaining relatively stable over time, yesterday's absurd is not always tomorrow's absurd. Mentalities change and so does the threshold of tolerance. With the advent on a large scale of digital animation capable of reproducing any impossibility, children are now accustomed from an early age to entering the world of the fantastic and the unreal.

# CHAPTER 11
# METAPHOR AND METONYMY

**A metaphor is the transfer of meaning between words or groups of words by analogy of situation or action.** We often speak of making an image, of pictorial language, for metaphorical discourse. The metaphor is the main compound of poetic speech, because it makes possible the flowering of language, and thus the transcending of flat reality into a symbolic universe. When used to make people laugh, the metaphor is the poetry of humour. Coupled with other processes, the metaphor articulates comic discourse as a whole. This is because the metaphor is almost second nature to humorous language.

I. Charles Henry Bennett, 1857, from Aesop (6th century BCE), *The Frog and the Ox*. All rights reserved.

# MIRA FALARDEAU

"Once a little Frog sat by a big Frog, by the side of a pool. 'Oh, father,' said he, 'I have just seen the biggest animal in the world; it was as big as a mountain, and it had horns on its head, and it had hoofs divided in two.'

'Pooh, child,' said the old Frog, 'that was only Farmer White's Ox. He is not so very big. I could easily make myself as big as he.' And he blew, and he blew, and he blew, and swelled himself out.

'Was he as big as that?' he asked the big Frog.

'Oh, much bigger,' said the little Frog.

The old Frog blew, and blew, and blew again, and swelled himself out, more than ever.

'Was he bigger than that?' he said.

'Much, much bigger,' said the little Frog.

'I can make myself as big,' said the old Frog. And once more he blew, and blew, and blew, and swelled himself out, and he burst!"

> Aesop built here a kind of classical schema of irony about the desire for power. To see this poor frog swelling inordinately, to see it swelling, swelling, swelling until it bursts, one cannot help thinking of all arrogant excesses of this world, such as the 2008 explosion of that famous real-estate bubble. The dialogue between the frog and its frog friend to see if the former will manage to overtake the ox shows just how pathetic disproportionate ambition can be.

Metaphors for the purpose of making people laugh, by transporting the subject to another universe, lighter in appearance, allows us to tackle subjects that are unbearable in real life. The simple game of transfer, by its very process, is fun. To move into the world of flavors, colors, music, animals, is a bit like changing floors to see the world from a different angle.

Metaphor is the culmination of comix discourse. In the typical allegory of fables, making animals speak like humans for a parodic purpose also has metaphorical resonances since fables are ironic about societies, both ancient and contemporary. Likewise, to schematize to the extreme a situation or the characteristics of a person gives a sort of concentrate of the whole, as if we were only showing immanence of beings and things. For centuries, this was seen in caricatures, the theater and all arts using comic language.

But in the 20th century, the rise of surrealism and nonsense in the performing arts and cinema has given a larger role to metaphorical discourse. As in minimalist art, where the languages of humour

# WHAT'S SO FUNNY?

always conceal a social critique. By rejecting the usual codes of discourse, the author signifies the denunciation of social conventions, civilized life's codes.

> Samuel Beckett, *Waiting for Godot,* comedy in two acts
> (1948–49), Act. 1.

ESTRAGON: Charming spot

(*He turns, advances, halts facing the audience.*)

Inspiring prospects. (*He turns to Vladimir.*) Let's go.

VLADIMIR: We can't.

E.: Why not?

V.: We're waiting for Godot.

E.: (*Despairingly*). Ah. (*Pause.*) You're sure it was here?

V.: What?

E.: That we were to wait.

V.: He said by the tree. (*They look at the tree.*) Do you see any others?

E.: What is it?

V.: I don't know. A willow.

E.: Where are the leaves?

V.: It must be dead.

E.: No more weeping.

V.: Or perhaps it's not the season.

E.: Looks to me more like a bush.

V.: A shrub.

E.: A bush.

V.: What are you insinuating? That we've come to the wrong place?

E.: He should be here.

# MIRA FALARDEAU

V.: He didn't say for sure he'd come.

E.: And if he doesn't come?

V.: We'll come back tomorrow.

> The success of this nihilistic theatrical work signed by the brilliant Irish writer Samuel Beckett (1906-1989) is first of all due to its extreme simplification of action which results in total non-action. These two beings lost in the immensity of the nothingness of life, waiting for someone they don't know, in a place they are not sure about, for perhaps the rest of their lives, are oscillating between comedy and drama. The tramps wander, saying nothing important, in a minimal setting waiting to be there no longer. Theater of the absurd, yes, but first and foremost theater of nothing, of nothingness symbolizing the human condition. Strangely, this extreme simplification of direction, setting and dialogue gives a disturbing intensity to the whole but at the same time, we laugh from the beginning to the end of the play, undoubtedly faced with the ambiguity between the comedy of the situation and the anguish generated by the nothingness of our lives. *Waiting for Godot* was Beckett's greatest success.

At the opposite pole of this kind of literature of the unspoken according to Beckett's own words (*Molloy*, 1951), metaphors can also transport you to a borderline oneiric dark and highly charged universe.

> Umberto Eco, *The Name of the Rose*, 1983, Seventh Day, Night.
> *(Jorge explains Aristotle's supposed aim in his -false- book on laughter here).*

"Jorge de Burgos — (The comedy) ... 'achieves the effect of the ridiculous by showing the defects and vices of ordinary men. Here, Aristotle sees the tendency to laughter as a force of good, which can also have an instructive value: through witty riddles and unexpected metaphors, though it tells us things differently from the way they are, as if it were lying, it actually obliges us to examine them closely'". (p. 276)

Here, Eco even gives us a key to the book *The Name of the Rose*, whose overall plot is metaphorical.

"(Jorge) 'But if one day, somebody, brandishing the words of the Philosopher and therefore speaking as a philosopher, were to raise the weapon of laughter to the condition of a subtle weapon, if the rhetoric of conviction were replaced by the rhetoric of mockery, if the topics of the patient construction of images of redemption were to be replaced by the topics of the impatient dismantling and upsetting of every holy and venerable image – oh, that day even you, William, and all your knowledge, would be swept away!'

# WHAT'S SO FUNNY?

Guillaume de Baskerville — 'Why, I would match my wit with the wit of others.'" (p. 278)

> A multitude of literary works have used metaphor for humorous purposes, but the Italian novelist and academic Umberto Eco (1932–2016) had the genius to approach the theoretical underpinnings of rhetoric and humour as a semiologist and then applied certain of these principles in his writing. Eco invents a fake book that Aristotle would have dedicated to laughter, a book that turns out to be poisoned, both literally and figuratively. *The Name of the Rose* is a remarkable metaphor uniting a labyrinthine library and knowledge, whose passages about laughter and religious faith harbour premonitory resonances. So, therefore, we find ourselves, thanks to Eco's incisive mind, in a metaphorical construction (the entire book) wherein the heart of the plot lies in a fictitious journey into the past in search of the rhetoric of derision. At the end of the novel, Eco offers a prodigious dialogue about laughter as a weapon between the hero Guillaume de Baskerville (named after one of Arthur Conan Doyle's Sherlock Holmes adventures: *The Hound of the Baskervilles*) and the dark guardian of the library, Jorge de Burgos, declaiming for page after page on the power of laughter. The crisis of the caricatures of Muhammad, with which we will deal later, embodies Eco's presentiments as expressed through the words of Jorge de Burgos.

Director Jean-Jacques Annaud realised an impressive movie, *The Name of the Rose* (1986) with Sean Connery, placing more emphasis on the plot's dark side. Eco, after the phenomenal success of the book, continued the parallel writing of scholarly texts and dense novels such as *Foucault's Pendulum* (1989) (*Il pendolo di Foucault*, 1988), satirizing exaggerated interpretations, sadly the order of the day in our 21$^{st}$ century. He published weightier texts but also some lighter ones such as *How to Travel with a Salmon and Other Essays* (1998), a hilarious collection of texts such as "Fragment", presented as an entry in an encyclopedia of anti-knowledge, in the manner of the Dadaists.

## Visual Metaphor

The visual metaphor, for its part, consists of a transfer of forms according to an association between two actions. The metaphorical transfer shows a scene which implies another. Symbolic caricatures in which the object of mockery comes across, for example, as a character of mythology are metaphorical. Cartoonists of the early satirical press made abundant use of references to mythology, addressing a literate public educated in Greco-Latin classics.

II. Honoré Daumier, *Europe on a Living Bomb*, circa 1850.

Daumier (1808-1879) in *Europe on a Living Bomb* speaks this language which became the basis of allegorical caricatures wherein the situation shown is read and decoded in the light of another situation familiar to readers. Daumier was here playing on the correspondence between the goddess Europa's imbalance on a bomb ready to explode and an imminent danger for Europe. Readers identify with the woman stretching out her arms to keep her balance, seeing themselves as citizens of this imperiled Europe, feeling the danger in their flesh. Since March 2022, Europeans have no doubt sometimes had the same feeling seeing Ukraine's invasion by Russia.

The 19$^{th}$ century saw the emergence of a quite free press, with the birth of many satirical newspapers in western countries, some of them copycat versions of others.

III. J. Walker, *Punch in Canada*, no 1, Jan. 1, 1849

## WHAT'S SO FUNNY?

IV. *Punch, London Charivari*, 1841, no.1

Preceded by the *Charivari Canadien* in 1844, *Punch in Canada*, in 1849, shows the Canadian cousin of the British *Punch* or *London Charivari* covered with winter clothes in an amusing allusion to our winter, blazing the trail for other satirical periodicals in America. The swirl of amusing illustrations of northern Canadian life found on the cover page, including the sign written in French (in fact Frenchifying Punch's name to "Monsieur Ponche") designating our friend's cabin (upper left), demonstrates here again the strong links between French and English in the English colony as in Townsend's caricature seen in Chapter 1. *Le Charivari* had been published in France as early as in 1832 by Philipon, whose irresistible King Louis Philippe pear we saw the in "Anthropomorphism" in Chapter 8, which was more oriented to social than to political critiques. Then, there was an irrepressible tidal wave which was going to sweep over the Western satirical world. We saw that *Punch*, sub-titled *The London Charivari*, arrived in London in 1841. And also, in 1847, in Berlin, came *Punsch*, followed by *Berliner Charivari* in 1847. The puppet figure of Punch, or Mister Punch of *Punch and Judy* shows, was directly inspired by a character of the commedia dell'arte, Pulcinella, the impertinent buffoon. Placing that figure of a servant of peasant origin, who was both rude and witty, on the frontispiece of satirical magazines featuring very strong and subtle critiques of politics and kings was quite ironical. With this understatement, new satirical magazines were implying: "Look how anybody, even the humblest, is able to see the absurdities of Nobles and Sovereigns." By shifting the point of view from the elite to the people, the publications were casting a harsh light on the actions of the Powerful. The door was open for metaphors adapted to specific cultures.

V. Anon., "Napoleon III cutting the German Cake",
*Punsch*, Germany, 1866.

This anonymous caricature dealing with German fears of a possible invasion by France depicts the French Emperor Napoleon III, heir to the disproportionate ambitions of his uncle, Napoleon I, as a pastry chef serving young Prussians pieces of the Germanic countries like an Emperor of the whole of Europe, which of course he was not. The feeling of being treated like pawns, little ones patiently waiting for their piece of the cake, is the image that emerges from this incisive and premonitory metaphor. That crisis involving Luxembourg, Belgium and several Germanic states was leading up to the Franco-German war of 1870, a conflict that Napoleon III lost miserably, precipitating his downfall.

With the 20$^{th}$ century, visual metaphors became the preferred weapon of critical humour. Contemporary humorous drawing has appropriated this process and one could almost say that the two words, metaphor and caricature, have become synonymous. Like verbal metaphors, visual metaphors sometimes flirt with the absurd, especially in the world humorous drawing, a branch of caricature, as we said, which stages ordinary people and not the Great of the world.

## WHAT'S SO FUNNY?

VI. Roland Topor, "Le pendu"(The Hanged Man),
circa 1960. All rights reserved.

The French cartoonist Topor (1938-1997) draws a tree on which a man has been hanged, but from above and upside down. We first think of the absurdity of the gesture, which resembles suicide. Then comes the idea that the soul of the deceased has ascended to heaven. And then, finally, and this is due to Topor's black humour, we end up laughing out loud faced with the absurdity of life.

Bold productions where each element of the decor refers to the decried situation are difficult to construct, so they are rare but even more eloquent. They often revolve in deep territories where the parable builds a parallel story that lightens the message, makes it more diffuse even if it is very weighty.

VII. Norman McLaren, *The Neighbours*, © NFB, 1952.

# MIRA FALARDEAU

*The Neighbours*, an Oscar-winning experimental film by Norman McLaren, is a parable which opens with the difficulty of getting along between neighbours and evolves into a vigorous plea against war. It is punctuated by "animated sound", discovered by McLaren, produced by images photographed on the soundtrack, generating otherworldly sounds which further add to the robotic demeanour of these two neighbors played by Jean-Paul Ladouceur and Grant Munro, who kill each other without pity. From the dispute over a simple flower located at the boundary of their two properties, the two protagonists come to blows, and gradually turn into monsters who do not hesitate to murder even a baby who happens to be there by chance, a scene that was expunged from the Oscar-winning version. The issue of the often-gratuitous and barbaric killing in war is evoked by a particular animation technique, "pixillation", which disembodies humans by filming them frame by frame, jerking their steps as if they were moving like robots. A monumental metaphor on the cruel absurdity of war, *The Neighbours* is a film that first makes spectators smile, then laugh, finally freezing us as we confront such utter desolation. Desolation due to any war, and to the total imbecility of its underlying motives.

Recently, a softer metaphoric style has reappeared in force in the many animated films abounding on screens of all kinds. Animation is no longer just a matter for children: following avant-garde animation aimed at an informed public, initially comprised largely of short films, there is now an entire sector of feature animation that has converted to mature discourse.

Peter Lord and Nick Park, *Chicken Run*, Aardman Studios, 2000.

Modeling clay animation is experiencing a revival with these two British artists, Peter Lord (1953- ) and Nick Park (1958- ), also the fathers of the Wallace and Gromit characters born in 1985. In *Chicken Run*, they have reconstructed a disturbing henhouse that looks like a concentration camp where hens, with affected British accents, are trying by all means to escape from this hell while the cruel owner Mrs. Tweedy concocts a Machiavellian plan to produce chicken pot pies! The anthropomorphic metaphor is embodied by speech with several voices, both light-hearted and ominous. Pungent criticism of the unimaginable cruelty of concentration camps, this satire is also a hymn to hope since the henhouse concludes its saga on a marvelous island where all is well that ends well.

One of the best examples of minimalist comic art is "intellectual comics", which often have metaphorical tones with their rejection of traditional comic book codes and their committed discourse. In 1950,

## WHAT'S SO FUNNY?

with his comic strip *Peanuts* (1950–2000), Charles Schulz (1922–2000) began to attribute to children the acts and anxieties of adults. He reaped phenomenal success because the allusion is double-edged: does he mean that children are wiser than adults or that adults act like children?

An absolute revolution in the language of comics, this intellectual tangent features individuals who dispassionately converse on the most diverse contemporary subjects as if they themselves were not personally involved. Their gestures and minimalist mimicry remain frozen, as if they were fascinated by their own discourse. This wave was followed by Johnny Hart (1931–2007) with *BC* (1958–2007) where, in a gag-a-day format, prehistoric characters, accompanied by animals each one wackier than the next, evolve with concerns strangely resembling ours. Hart wanted to demonstrate the constancy of human feelings through the ages. He occasionally placed objects evoking modern society in his strips as if he wanted people to think his contemporaries often behave like prehistoric men. From the 1980s, by displaying his Christian faith, he turned his back on Jewish and Muslim readers who often forced him to withdraw particular jokes. For example, his 1996 and 2001 Easter gags sparked a large number of complaints, initiating a new era of media control by readers and viewers, the effects of which we are only just beginning to measure.

This particular genre of visual satire is in play on this immediately perceptible metaphorical level, where contestation is indicated by a systematic rejection of certain codes of discourse to arrive at an extremely stripped-down image. A crowd of creators will reject one or more of the codes of language, down to a minimalist situation where two people converse without any other action than the passage of time. "Intellectual comics" often have two people sitting face to face and make them talk on the most unusual subjects, both to ironize empty discourse and to illustrate the immobility of certain mind-sets.

VIII. Nicole Hollander, *"What does the job entail?"*
*I'm training to be tall and blonde*, Saint Martins Press, 1979.

Just from the appearance of Hollander's strips, we immediately understand why the lyrics completely invade the universe of the characters, who are drowned by their own words. Immobilism is a constant of intellectual comics and the absence of movement in an art of movement here means a refusal of the rules. Without the usual outline of the balloon, the texts of the bubbles spread throughout the box, thoughts and dialogues forming a sea of letters, more or less drowning out the anti-misogynistic theme. Logorrhea envelops the characters like a mask that stifles their feelings.

Underground comics played with these same metaphorical tones, but this time at the opposite pole of minimalism.

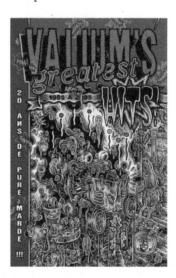

IX. Henriette Valium, Cover of *Valium's Greatest Hits*, 2014.

133

## WHAT'S SO FUNNY?

> Valium (pseud. Patrick Henley) is undoubtedly one of the most valiant representatives of this wave with his latest works. Boxes overflow with greasy lines including pornographic or intestinal hints. Creatures with bulging eyes typical of hallucinogenic overdoses wander around making scandalous remarks written in dripping typography, reinforced by their coarse gestures, all contributing to manifest this generation's disgust with the standardized life of their parents' generation.

Metaphors invite a rapprochement between two universes in order to help us understand an event otherwise difficult to comprehend.

X. Art Spiegelman, *Maus II: A Survivor Tale: And Here My Troubles Began*, p. 42, four boxes. [1]

**1st box**: a journalist-dog wearing a mask (symbolising Americans) and a wig interviews the author-mouse (wearing a mouse mask symbolising Jews) sitting at his drawing table. Behind the journalist, a cameraman-dog. At the right of the image, stands a journalist-cat (wearing a cat mask, representing Germans). At their feet, a mass grave of dead lying pell-mell, recalling images of the Holocaust's mass murder and graves.

---

[1] Graphic Novel Excerpt from THE COMPLETE MAUS: A SURVIVOR'S TALE by Art Spiegelman, Maus, Volume I copyright © 1973, 1980, 1981, 1982, 1983, 1984, 1985, 1986 by Art Spiegelman; Maus, Volume II copyright © 1986, 1989, 1990, 1991 by Art Spiegelman. Used by permission of Pantheon Books, an imprint of the Knopf Doubleday Publishing Group, a division of Penguin Random House LLC. All rights reserved.

# MIRA FALARDEAU

**Text:**

American journalist — *Tell our viewers what message you want them to get from your book?*

Art — *A message? I dunno…*

**2nd box:** the mass grave has disappeared and the journalist-cat on the left speaks.

Art — *I-I never thought of reducing it to a message. I mean. I wasn't trying to CONVINCE anybody of anything. I just wanted-*

German journalist (interrupting) – *Your book is being translated into German…*

**3rd box:** The exchange continues between him and the author. The only allusion to mass graves is a fly hovering.

German journalist – *Many younger Germans have had it up to HERE with holocaust stories. These things happened before they were even born. Why should they feel guilty?*

Art – *Who am I to say?…*

**4th box:** a third journalist, a Jew-mouse wearing a kind of pyjama appears at the right, pushing the American journalist out. The author-mouse (Art) seems exhausted.

Art – *But a lot of the corporations that flourished in Nazi Germany are richer than ever. I dunno…Maybe EVERYONE has to feel guilty. EVERY-ONE! FOREVER!*

The Jewish journalist – *Okay…Let's talk about Israel…*

When the American Art Spiegelman (1948- ) recounts the nightmare of a Jew in Mauschwitz by staging the action of mice (the Jews) and cats (the Nazis), he helps to lift the veil on this unfathomable story of the Shoah. As we know that cats and mice are part of two different worlds but also of a shared world and that their languages are totally opposite, we will probably better understand this paradox of human cruelty toward their fellow human beings. A graphic novel translated into thirty languages and the first Pulitzer-Prize-winning comic strip (1992), *Maus* impresses the reader with its astonishing way of telling the story of concentration-camp survivor Vladek as narrated by his son Art, the author of the comic strip. The tone of woodcut on a black background, with a marked screen, depicts a sordid atmosphere. The entire backdrop is metaphorical. Each group is represented by a different kind of animal: behind cats and mice, there are the Polish-pigs, the American-dogs, the

## WHAT'S SO FUNNY?

French-frogs, the British-fishes and the Swedish-moose. The choice of each breed of animal was made according to a particular logic, namely the supposed wickedness of the pigs, certain Poles having persecuted the Jews; or favorite foods according to nationality: frogs for the French and fish for the British; or an animal icon of the country like the moose for the Swedes... Art Spiegelman invites us to witness a metaphorical feat which we are going to observe more closely. A second discourse unfolds parallel to the whole horrible history of the Holocaust, wherein Spiegelman constructs a *mise-en-abyme* by telling us the story of the story, that is to say the epic efforts he had to deploy to achieve the narration of his father, an unpredictable and hypochondriac character. The second volume, from which the analysed extract is taken, was published a few years (1991) after the first (1980 in the magazine *Raw*, 1986 as an album), offering us the shock of Spiegelman confronted with celebrity, and his self-criticism and doubts in relation to his decidedly introspective approach. The self-mockery here reaches new heights: with an unconcealed cord to tie their masks, he disguises the characters of his interview as a mouse for him and the Jewish journalist, as a cat for the German journalist, and as a dog for the American one. The transposition of his characters into animals, the central metaphor of his story, is, by the masks tied at the back of their heads with a very visible lace, thus multiplied by two. The fact that the tie is so visible can be interpreted as our difficulty in disguising the cultural weight that we carry. This is like a metaphor within a metaphor. Spiegelman also gives us one of the keys to decoding this scene, alluding to the ethnic origin of the protagonists of the interview, acting like judges, especially the American (dog) journalist wearing a kind of wig perhaps evoking Nuremberg judges. The American wants to know the "message", the German recalls the innocence of today's young Germans, while the Jew seems to want to decide on the scope of the work as a whole, browbeating the poor author bereft of arguments yet concluding: "Maybe everyone has to feel guilty. All! For all time!" These narrative acrobatics are certainly not unrelated to the book's immense success, Spiegelman allowing us to enter the work which calls his own approach into question.

As if censorship no longer knew what prey to go after in these times of "cancel culture", it was reported (by CBC News, on Jan. 28, 2022) that in January 2022, a Tennessee school district voted to ban *Maus* because of its "inappropriate language and nudity". The following day Spiegelman's graphic novel shot up to the top 20 best-sellers on Amazon.com!

### Visual Metonymy

**Metonymy is a metaphorical process by which meaning is transferred between two concepts united by a necessary relationship, such as the cause for the effect, the content for**

**the container, the part for the whole.** The metonymic figure of the **synecdoche** more precisely indicates the part for the whole or vice versa and any variation of this type as the genus for the species. Everyday discourse is full of these amusing metonymies that have become so commonplace that they go almost unnoticed, such as "Are we going to eat a bite?" to invite someone to share a meal or "Shall we have a beer?" which is often an invitation to share the whole six-pack or spend the evening at the bar! In everyday life, we often speak by metonymy because it is a quick and effective way of expressing ourselves. In the language of allegory and humor, metonymy is commonly used for designation in general. The whole essence of symbolic language lies in this ability to transfer a concept into an encompassing word or phrase, for example, the crown for the king, or the hammer and sickle for communism.

An amusing variation of synecdoche is **assemblage**, a visual process whereby the joining of kindred elements creates an ensemble whose silhouette evokes the whole from which these parts come.

XI. Giuseppe Arcimboldo, "The Librarian", painting, 16th c. All rights reserved.

Giuseppe Arcimboldo (1527-1593), a Milanese Mannerist painter, revived and transformed the technique the Ancients had of creating masks from floral or other

## WHAT'S SO FUNNY?

vegetal elements, mainly in Dionysian cults. Arcimboldo made fanciful assemblages and drew striking portraits. Around 1562, he began to develop comic portraits, the "ghiribizzi" in which he would playfully assemble fruits, vegetables and plants to symbolize the seasons. He would also juxtapose animals or objects, such as this librarian whose assembled books of diverse dimensions create the character. If we take the assemblage at face value, we can say here that the very essence of the librarian is in fact the books he cherishes to the point of becoming them. Arcimboldo thus set the stage for various trades (the Cook, the Gardener), the seasons (Autumn, Spring), the elements (Water, Fire) and with incredible verve would meld the shapes of plants, objects and utensils into fabulous humanoids that have been called "composite heads", akin to caricature.

This game was brought back into fashion by the surrealists of the early 20$^{th}$ century, who loved all kinds of word and image games. Sometimes cartoonists use assemblage in a metaphorical way to mean that the whole does not exist apart from all its parts.

XII. Hans-Georg Rauch, "Portrait of Mao", 1970. All rights reserved.

The German cartoonist Rauch (1939-1993) published humorous drawings in German and international newspapers such as *Der Spiegel* and *The New York Times*. He chose here to ridicule the supreme leader by forming his portrait through an assemblage of a Chinese multitude. The crowd recreates Mao's features as if on a television screen, shaping the facial contours with highlights and shadows. Shivers ripple us as we face the chilling homogeneity of the people of this immense country. The great dictator appears as a precarious shadow existing only by means of the masses.

The tones of metonymy are often discreet, self-effacing; they comprise an understatement that says less to signify more.

XIII. Tim *(Crying)*, 1970. All rights reserved.

Drawing for the French magazine *L'Express*, Tim (1919-2002) (pseud. Louis Mitelberg), a cartoonist and sculptor of Polish origin, created a famous image based on a powerful metonymy: with characteristic superimposed lines, he drew the large full face of an Asian woman whose crying eyes are in the shape of airplanes dropping bombs. So, sobs, the effect, are represented by their cause, B-52 bombers. The stasis of the scene as well as its mute side, no words to support the discourse of the image, combine to transmit a powerful message.

Is it funny? No. But let's not forget the paradoxical interpenetration of humour and tragedy. While black humour can desensitise us in the face of drama, committed humour, as here, makes it possible to engage in something like respectful meditation in front of horror, but in a more subtle way than a denunciatory text would.

Metonymy plays in the field of the implied, and can even stem from the temptation of self-censorship. Plantu gives a good example in *Le Monde*.

## WHAT'S SO FUNNY?

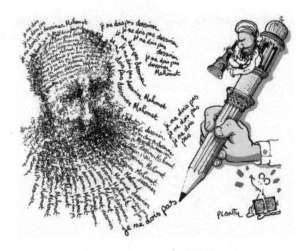

XIV. Plantu, *Je ne dois pas dessiner Mahomet*
(I must not draw Muhammad), *Le Monde*, 2006.

> Plantu (pseud. Jean Plantureux, 1951- ) was editorial cartoonist for the newspaper *Le Monde* between 1972 and 2021. In reference to the crisis provoked by the caricatures of Muhammad, he published this caricature formed of the sentence "I must not draw Muhammad". It should be noted that for contemporary Muslims, it is considered blasphemy to show the face of the Prophet, even if historically, this has not always been the case. The lines of Plantu's handwriting, which intersect more or less densely, generate the framework in which the reader vaguely makes out the turbaned head of a heavily bearded man, an allusion to the "bearded ones", a nickname given in France to Islamic fundamentalists. The pencil-minaret adds by its comical double meaning to the confused sensation of a double discourse. The fact of saying and not saying at the same time reflects the constraints imposed by newspaper owners and editors who no longer dared to allow their columnists and cartoonists to deal with the subject of fundamentalists and the Muhammad cartoons when cartoonists were threatened with death or even killed for having caricatured the Prophet. We will see that the situation has gone from bad to worse. In 2006, Plantu founded the association "Cartooning for Peace", bringing together around two hundred cartoonists from all over the world for the purpose of defending freedom of expression through caricature.

It is appropriate here to dwell for a moment on the facts surrounding "the affair of the Muhammad cartoons", which deeply disturbed the community of cartoonists almost everywhere on the planet. And which continues to do so.

## MIRA FALARDEAU

## The Metaphor in the Service of Freedom of Speech

On January 19, 2022, *The Comics Journal* published an article signed by Matthias Wivel under the title of *"Westergaard and the World's Most Notorious Cartoon"* on the occasion of the death of the artist. In fact, Kurt Westergaard was the author of one of the famous twelve cartoons published in the Danish daily *Jyllands-Posten* on September 30, 2005. The one which went around the world, called "Bomb in the Turban", shows the Prophet with a black beard, cruel eyes surmounted by charcoal-colored eyebrows, topped by a dark turban bearing an inscription in Arabic proclaiming his faith in Islam and a lit bomb capping the whole thing.

Subsequently, from 2005 to 2007, tempers flared. Faced with the unleashing of Muslim fundamentalism denouncing these caricatures, both in Europe and in the countries of the Maghreb and the Middle East, where dozens of people were dying in violent demonstrations, European satirical publications, including *Charlie Hebdo*, reprinted the cartoons, adding their own cartoons, as a gesture of tribute. At that time, the pressure then rose a notch and the Muslim world treated the authors of these drawings as renegades. In 2008, the bombing of the Swedish embassy in Islamabad left eight dead and several injured. Cyberattacks and the ransacking of the *Charlie Hebdo* magazine headquarters in 2011 raised the temperature of confrontation a degree. Opponents went on the direct attack. But for *Charlie Hebdo,* which has embodied the tradition of disrespectful mockery since its founding in 1970, freedom of speech has no limit. Because it continued to publish antireligious cartoons, fanatics saw this as a provocation demanding dramatic action.

Indeed, on January 7, 2015, three Muslim fundamentalists entered the editorial offices of this satirical left-wing Parisian magazine and killed twelve journalists, collaborators and guards with Kalashnikovs, shouting "Allah Akbar". Five eminent caricaturists were killed in cold blood: Cabu, Charb, Wolinski, Tignous and Honoré. Charb was particularly targeted, as editor and author of cartoons of Muhammad deemed blasphemous by fundamentalists who had repeatedly threatened him with death. The immediate effect was a feeling of horror at these murders and the whole community tightened up; a monster demonstration for freedom of expression and against fundamental-

141

## WHAT'S SO FUNNY?

ists took place on January 11 in Paris, in which 44 heads of state from all over the world participated.

The slogan "I am Charlie" went viral while that of "I am not Charlie" showed up in support of the other side. Demonstrations applauding the assassinations took place in several cities in the Middle East and the Maghreb. The next issue of *Charlie Hebdo* sold eight million copies, whereas the circulation before the events was only ten thousand. Exhibitions planning to showcase *Charlie Hebdo* drawings were canceled. On the other hand, debates on freedom of expression, caricature and blasphemy were flourishing on numerous platforms, unleashing torrents of opinions. Some humorous authors and caricaturists admitted that they would never express their ideas in the same way again.

Many cartoonists admitted that they no longer cared to caricature Muhammad. Opinion was now divided into the "I am Charlie", the "I am not Charlie", and also the "I am Charlie, but" camps.

Why not take a moment to reflect on this historic moment when caricatures dramatically found themselves at the center of the news? So, how did the grotesque and vaguely insulting drawings intended for the irreligious readers of *Charlie Hebdo* come to arouse such fury among Muslim fundamentalists? Reading Wivel's article reminds us of some facts that have been well known to scholars from the outset, but which bear emphasizing because they shed new light on the whole dynamic surrounding this story's origins in Denmark. Seen from a certain angle, we understand that the initial publication of the "Muhammad cartoons" could pass for provocation.

If Westergaard was openly on the left, manifestly atheistic and in tune with liberal thought advocating tolerance and multiculturalism, the profile was different for the newspaper in which he published his caricature. The *Jyllands-Posten* newspaper was already known for its conservative, quasi-reactionary stance, whose core readership was the anti-immigration, particularly Islamophobic sector of the middle class, drawn to the right-wing Danish People's Party. It was the editorial staff of the newspaper that "ordered" these twelve anti-Muslim cartoons with the barely veiled aim of offending. Westergaard's caricature was undoubtedly the most explosive one of the lot, hence its immense impact would force him to live under surveillance for the rest of his life after an attempted attack on his home in 2010 by a Somali Islamist activist.

142

We are now witness to a total upheaval of values in the world of critical humour, in the aftermath of the January 2015 terrorist attacks in Paris. These assassinations of collaborators on a publication whose trademark is vitriolic humour were felt viscerally by the entire community of critical-humour cartoonists and journalists as an attack on each and every one of them; *Charlie Hebdo* has consequently become for them almost a symbol of freedom of expression. Their solidarity, accentuated by the Internet's allowing everyone to follow the work of their colleagues on a daily basis, was expressed by a surge of drawings in defense of *Charlie*. Even if most of them did not share the weekly's extreme views, they felt a collective responsibility to react.

XV. André-Philippe Côté, "Charlie",
*Le Soleil, Le Courrier International*, Jan. 8, 2015.

André-Philippe Côté (1955- ), a cartoonist with a background in comics and illustration, has been an editorial cartoonist for the daily *Le Soleil* from Quebec City since 1997. Here he situates the aggression and the response that cartoonists around the world felt and expressed in the face of the violent attack on *Charlie*. Threatened in the exercise of his profession, the artist then mirrors the position of his vis-à-vis, hands ready to grab his weapons in reply. This is what the artist is doing both literally and figuratively, his drawings poised to answer the assault. He dramatizes the aggression against caricaturists around the world and their response in the face of the murderous onslaught against *Charlie*. In a standoff, wired to the limit, the cartoonist and the terrorist size each other up. From the double meaning between forms and uses of pencil and weapon, both oblong-shaped tools, our gaze slides towards the metaphor where draftsman morphs into warrior.

## WHAT'S SO FUNNY?

This is where metaphor emerges front and centre. During the month of January 2015, cartoonists from throughout the so-called free world sprang into action, creating more and more powerful metaphors. Becoming a veritable leitmotiv, the pencil imposed itself as a symbol of resistance in a classic visual double meaning. In a metaphorical allusion to the 2001 terrorist attack, we had already seen several cartoonists turn the towers of New York's World Trade Center into giant pencils. In the defense of *Charlie*, the pencil imposed itself again as a leitmotiv from the visual double meaning between pencil and weapon, with the shift taking place metaphorically towards the "mise en scène" wherein the artist is shown as warrior.

Then the game calmed down somewhat and everyone went back to their business. But slowly, we realize that there are two fairly distinct large groups. Those who stood up. And the silent ones, who either out of fear or conviction or a bit of both, crouched and said nothing. A lull set in, and the horizon cleared.

Yet the assaults continued. On February 14, 2015, during a conference at the Krudttonden Cultural Center in Oosterbro near Copenhagen in tribute to the victims of *Charlie* entitled "Art, Blasphemy and Freedom of Expression" which was attended by the artist Lars Vilks, right-wing cartoonist, author of a 2007 cartoon in a Swedish newspaper of Muhammad with a dog's head, a shooting occurred, resulting in one death. The perpetrator of the shooting, claiming to be from the Islamic State (ISIS), was shot dead. On May 5, 2015, ISIS moved to American soil, this time striking by the hand of two young fundamentalists who opened fire at an exhibition of cartoons "against the prophet" in the Curtis Culwell Center, in Garland, Texas. The terrorists, identified on the radio as "soldiers of the caliphate" of the Islamic State, were killed on the spot at this strange competition organized by a group of far-right provocateurs, the Islamophobic association American Freedom Defense Initiative.

And finally, on October 16, 2020, horror takes another step forward. In the middle of a street in a suburb of Paris, a French teacher, Samuel Paty, who had shown the famous "caricatures of Muhammad" in his high-school class, was coldly beheaded by a fundamentalist, who was killed by police a few minutes after the attack. The teacher had shown the cartoons in a lesson on freedom of expression, having made the effort to allow students who might be offended by the images to leave the classroom.

MIRA FALARDEAU

## The Globalization of Humour

The globalization of this crisis, due in large part to the Internet, was extremely damaging to the world of cartooning in general. As Wivel (2022) so aptly puts it: "What the cartoon crisis reminded us of, however, is that such publication today is never merely local and that power relations change in a globalized context."

If we want to schematize, let's say that during much of the 20th century, things went like this: either, cartoonists worked for major newspapers read by cohorts of loyal subscribers and a broader public, congenially sharing kindred viewpoints; there were right-wing newspapers, center-right newspapers and center-left ones, and everyone knew which brand was what. Or, with regard to the sharp edges of the political prism, such as extreme right and left, the cartoonists of these restricted publications, often weekly newspapers or magazines, had their readers already won over to their causes. Of course, there were sometimes skirmishes between certain curious readers who went to see what cartoonists in the opposing camp were up to, but by and large, it was "everyone in their own camp".

This fine balance exploded with the arrival of social media and ultra-fast and international Internet exchanges. Overnight, in the first years of the 21st century, a new universe was being built where readers and ideological movements from all corners of the planet have access to the sites of satirical magazines where all the drawings are freely accessible. They would find themselves in a community of like-mindedness or at loggerheads in this virtual space called cyberspace. Far from being the only victims, cartoonists, by the very nature of their critical discourse now easily accessible with the click of a button and often without words, have found themselves on the front line, their drawings showcased and shared exponentially, most of the time without their consent. The publishers of mostly virtual magazines and newspapers no longer have their say and the drawings now travel without borders and without laws. This partly explains the immense hubbub caused

# WHAT'S SO FUNNY?

by the caricatures of Muhammad, far from being the only such event. Obviously, we have deliberately omitted describing in detail the situation in dictatorships, where the exercise of caricature has always been a high-flying sport. For example, and without wanting to dwell on this scandalous episode targeting the profession within a dictatorship, we remember with horror August 2011 when a Syrian cartoonist, Ali Ferzat, was beaten up and had both his hands broken because of a cartoon mocking Syrian president Bachar el-Assad.

During the decade of 2010–20, we witnessed a polarization of mentalities. On the right, a conservative position: often against abortion, gay marriage, trade unionism, immigration, nationalizations, social programs, and for traditional, family, religious, individualistic values. On the left, a mind-set open to new values: alter-globalism, ecology, protection of the environment, acceptance of immigrants and migrants, equality of men and women. If we want to add nuances, we find on the right a strong "libertarian" movement which, as its name suggests, advocates total individual freedom, implying an almost total withdrawal of the state from private enterprise and public affairs. On the left, the cards have been shuffled and "cancel culture" is strangely wreaking havoc on the very principle of freedom of expression. Its goal is to delete from public space "reprehensible" cultural expression. Obviously, there are many nuances in this concept of any "reprehensible". Hot-button issues such as systemic racism, ecological peril, gender-based violence, have pride of place in the debate, and "woke" thought, which means "a sharp awareness of social and racial inequalities", creates a kind of censorship despite all its good intentions.

Let us look more closely at this trend of thought. Initially, this movement is one of "purification" of social and cultural space. Let's see just how toxic this culture can be in a specific case of book-banning in the world of humour, more precisely in the world of comics. The event recounted here could be taken from a comedy, it is so extraordinary in its zaniness. But it really happened, with all the seriousness of a purification ceremony.

A news item released in September 2021 on the Radio-Canada website by the journalist Thomas Gerbet went around the world, igniting social networks and the mainstream press alike. It reported that in 2019, around thirty books for young people were burned in an auto-da-fe carried out in the jurisdiction of the Catholic School Council of Providence, Ontario, during a rite of "purification" per-

146

formed on the initiative of Ms. Suzy Kies. Among these books were *Tintin* and *Asterix* comics deemed racist in their depiction of indigenous peoples. Pretending to be an "indigenous knowledge keeper", Ms. Kies was advising schools run by the School Council. This news aroused high cries in the international community, especially in the world of comic book readers. Ms. Kies, then co-chair of the Native Commission, was later fired as much for her drastic advice as for the fact that she was not Native at all. Cancel culture has here gone beyond the limits of social acceptability, recalling the outer limits of proscription.

Such currents of thought have been crystallized in what we call cyberwarfare. We can add to these opinions various nuances of tolerance or intolerance depending on cultural traditions, authoritarian or liberal policies, as well as on alliances forged among religious, cultural or national groups. What was believed to be part of the world of science fiction becomes very real when malicious actors financed by obscure entities, where some observers recognize the profile of Russian or Chinese cyberattacks, are conveying ad infinitum their half-truths or out-and-out disinformation with malevolent intent.

This is how movements such as QAnon, a far-right conspiratorial movement originating in the United States but extended worldwide between the years 2017 and 2022, are taken over by trolls who proclaim their lies without respite. And it is in this way that the editors of newspapers and magazines are trapped. Faced with this unwelcome deluge of hundreds or more emails, in the mailboxes of their cartoonists and columnists, discouraged by criticism or even direct or indirect threats, editors become so unnerved that they begin to fear any criticism at all. Caricature, by its visual and easily transferable nature, becomes an art of the instantaneous in this new international borderless space.

For example, two crucial cases of censorship in the world of Western cartooning have taken place recently which confirm the vigor of this war of mentalities. And in both cases, the symbol used was the person of Trump, which cannot be a coincidence when you know the polarization this demagogic politician has caused and will surely cause again. We can readily extrapolate that supporters of this conservative ideology who occupy decision-making positions in the management of certain media have found it more convenient to silence cartoonists than to encourage public debate.

XVI. Michael de Adder,
*"Do you mind if I play through?" Brunswick News,* June 26, 2019.

The first case is that of the Canadian cartoonist Michael de Adder (1967- ). In June 2019, the *Brunswick News* press group based in New Brunswick ceased a 17-year collaboration with this freelance cartoonist, the day after the cartoon was published. The press group denied having fired him for this reason. But their denial is hard to believe. The incriminating cartoon shows the president of the United States, Donald Trump, as renowned for his lack of knowledge of international politics as for his passion for golf, which he shamelessly indulges in instead of seriously considering affairs of state, naturally, playing golf, oblivious to the fate of a migrant child lying at his feet. It is obviously necessary to know the referent of this small body: it is the corpse of a three-year-old Syrian boy, Alan Kurdi, discovered on a beach after the sinking of the boat he and other migrants had embarked on, fleeing deadly wars and dictatorships in search of a better life in the West. The metaphor makes Trump's golf course a global land space so, life is a game, nothing really matters, and he addresses the boy without noticing that he is dead. This is a reflection on Trump's indifference to the misery of migrants against whom, among other things, he started construction of a wall at the Mexican border designed to keep them out of the United States. De Adder's bushy style, wherein the lines intersect densely to generate dark shadows, accentuates the gravity of the message. In March 2021, he became a cartoonist at the American *Washington Post*. As of 2022, his signature has appeared in the *Toronto Star*.

A second event is also at the centre of a wave of silencing critical thought in caricature. The *New York Times International* had for several years been systematically republishing cartoons from almost everywhere on the planet, thus offering great visibility to the artists chosen. In 2021, incredible though it may seem, the news outlet stopped publishing all cartoons, in reaction to the outcry caused by single one. Thus, a media of paramount importance for cartoonists around the world who had seen their cartoons reproduced for a very wide audience suddenly ceased publishing them altogether! The world of cartooning was flabbergasted. The trigger was the republishing of a caricature by the Portuguese cartoonist Antonio Moreira Antunes, accused of anti-Semitism.

THE NEW YORK TIMES INTERNATIONAL EDITION

XVII. Antonio Moreira Antunes, "Canine Peace",
*The New York Times International Edition*, April 25, 2019.

The Portuguese artist Antonio Moreira Antunes' cartoon features then-President Trump wearing a yarmulke, walking his dog whose head is that of Netanyahu with a Star of David collar. We stand in front of a President of the United States, who does not know where he is going, leading by the nose, or rather the leash, the Israeli Prime Minister; unless it is the other way around, and it is the dog guiding its walker. Antonio's acid colors give a thundering, almost wacky tone to his criticism. This set fire to the powder keg, the critics accusing him of an anti-Semitic caricature. However, according to Antonio, his intention was far removed from this mentality. As he explained in an interview with Quentin Girard on June 2019 in *Libération*, the drawing had first been published in the Portuguese newspaper *Expresso* without causing a storm. He added that the title of the cartoon, "Canine Peace" ("La paix canine"), was omitted in the reissue. He claimed that he only wanted, in his allegori-

## WHAT'S SO FUNNY?

cal "mise en scène", to criticize the Netanyahu government's policy of annexation and the Trump government's decision in November 2020 to move its embassy from Tel Aviv to Jerusalem (thus granting recognition to Jerusalem as the capital, in defiance of international law). For him, the use of the kippa or the Star of David is not anti-Semitic but simply symbolic and customary. "The cartoon tells a story", he explained: "that of a blind man led by a guide dog".

Here is the foundation of the visual metaphor: showing a scene in action that refers transparently to another scene, mental this time. The problem here is obviously the referents which can shock in one case and go after approval and laughter in the other. Indeed, according to the *Washington Post* (Morton, 2019), Antonio, as he signs, was not new to anti-Semitic cartooning, hence the reaction of the *New York Times*. In 1983, he had even won a prize at the International Cartoon Festival of the Humour Pavilion in Montreal with a caricature reusing the famous photo of a Jewish child raising his hands in the Warsaw ghetto in 1943, to compare the position of Israel to that of Nazi Germany. This caused an outcry among Canadian and American Jewish associations. In any event, it is to a completely different reading of this case of censorship that the *Washington Post* invites us in its clarification, reminding us that a cartoonist's professional history can shed light on his true intentions. Or perhaps quite simply, is it the problem of decoding a caricature when it goes off to play in troubled territories where standoffs are exacerbated: on anti-Semitism, racism, violence against women, homophobia, etc.

As history is being written before our eyes, it is almost impossible for the historian to have the perspective necessary to describe even schematically current ideological movements. It is an understatement to say that nowadays, cartoonists and humorists of all kinds work in opaque territory. The war in Ukraine, which began in March 2022, and the war in Gaza in 2023–24, reveal a hardening of positions: some countries align themselves according to their economic interests, others along political, and still others along religious lines. A maelstrom of opinions is being created, and very astute are those who can guess in which direction "political correctness" will take cartoonists and humorists in the so-called "free" world a few years hence.

In the world of humour, the language used by artists can be daring in the extreme; they walk on a tightrope where, in principle, everything can be said because thereon lies what is funny, thereon

150

occurs the comic tension. Caricaturists, stage and screen comedians, frequently stand on the rope and in the line of fire at the same time.

To conclude this chapter on visual metaphor, let us not forget that this territory is specific to cartoonists and humorists: in the domain of metaphor, the language of distancing is spoken, which they put on like a second skin, disguising their discourse. For better and for worse.

# CONCLUSION
# TOWARDS A HUMOROUS SOCIETY?

**M**aintaining our hard-earned freedom of expression is the first priority. Our stroll through the evolution of comic processes has shown the extraordinary creativity of artists and authors of humour throughout the centuries. But beware: yellow light. Since the advent of the Web and social media, languages have been disrupted by total interbreeding.

At the dawn of the 3rd millennium, with the proliferation of media platforms, the fight for ratings has given rise to various experiments to increase audiences. The concept of a "humorous society", set forth, let us recall, by Lipovetsky challenges us. Humour, or rather comedy, is everywhere: public affairs broadcasts, shows or talk shows, and multiple websites. Mutations progress so fast that analysis has a hard time keeping up. Yes, current humorous processes are the same as ancient ones but sometimes their critical capacity seems reduced, as if their sole purpose was to elicit a good laugh. Clairvoyant would be the one able to predict the nature of critical humour arts, thirty years from now!

Clues are piling up to stimulate our vigilance. Mixing genres between private and public humour, continued decline in the range and number of traditional media and of the critically-minded columnists who have taken pride therein, notable thinning out of political humour, instant knee-jerk reactions via social media to comedians and caricaturists, cancel culture, polarization of political discourse: let's take a closer look at the dangers we are facing.

## WHAT'S SO FUNNY?

One of the most visible revolutions is certainly the shift to the Web for reading. As a result, subscriptions to newspapers and magazines have undergone a vertiginous plunge, and reading on paper is now an activity in free fall. Therefore, whether in the caricature, the comic strip or irreverent chronicle, are virtual magazine and newspaper websites going to have the same satirical power? And how are they going to survive the free access new audiences demand?

The situation is changing in most daily newspapers: their websites increasingly present editorial cartoons produced by several different artists. The post of editorial cartoonist for one particular daily is slowly disappearing. The dominant trend is one of economy and in the United States, for example, more and more agencies are selling the same cartoon to hundreds of newspapers. Now, if one cartoonist's discourse displeases the editorial staff, it is so easy: they simply do not call him or her back! Indeed, much as local cartooning has managed to maintain its role of watchdog, both on municipal and regional subjects concerning the environment, official corruption or other hot topics of the moment, a cartoon read by millions of readers scattered everywhere is necessarily more global, not to say less combative. The critical function is thereby often dethroned, leaving in its place mere amusement.

Regarding oral and textual humour, the Cultural Revolution years from 1960 to 1980 gave rise to humorists with acerbic and pointed political criticism. But one has the impression that the new generation of comedians, the one now filling public venues and websites, has fewer political concerns. As if "brainy criticism" were their fathers' or grandfathers' business, now outdated, and replaced by more everyday, often spicier, themes.

The current shift from private to semi-public, and especially from private to public, satire through social media is just one of the complex facets of new media. Indeed, if at a private party I make fun of my neighbour, of his nose or of his religious, political or other behaviour, and an ill-intentioned guest film or records me without my knowledge and then openly circulates my mockery, he has distorted my humour. In addition to the underhandedness, a private comic speech has been transformed, a message intended just for my close "friends", into a public denunciation. The culprit becomes a broadcaster of my mockery for a purpose larger than mine, which was simply to have fun. It is as if the discreet graffiti about Rufus seen in Chapter 1 has ended up in the public square of Pompeii! Here again, two possible outcomes: if the person mocked is totally unknown, the harm, albeit unfortunately, would be limited to this person and their own circle. Human tragedies are taking place nowadays by means of the immense potential of social media; young people are particularly fragile in the face of possible slippages. On the other hand, if the person mocked is a public figure, the damage caused by slander or defamation would be proportional to the notoriety of the subject. The result would look more like a sitcom than a critique of ideas. Is it left-wing, right-wing, center? This kind of mockery does not specify it often!

Funnier inventions can be found on websites like You Tube or Tik Tok, where, among other things, anyone can install their homemade video. But here we find ourselves in front of the antithesis of universal discourse; as its name indicates, a homemade video is someone's little film, intended for restricted distribution. Yet sometimes a flash of genius makes a video go viral, and then half of the Internet audience watch it and laugh. Here, the wacky wins.

Several websites of zany scenarios taken from daily life also exist, and the fact that most of the time we don't know if these are truly spontaneous jokes or entirely staged scenes changes absolutely nothing. Such sketches most often belong to the world of private laughter. Here, neither condensation, nor other humorous process, nor critical intention: most often the happenchance of a goof or an unfortunate blunder. This is pure comedy but totally innocuous because involuntary. A bit like the programs tracking unfortunate passers-by on the street, setting them up and filming them during the catch. Even if politicians or jet-set stars are the pranksters. In fact, it is almost pathetic to see politicians clowning around like this. Here is the world upside down. Supreme inversion where the mocked mock themselves to stop others from doing it!

For the moment, we are witnessing authorial transfers directly to the Web. But who can guarantee that media will be able to resist over time, as fashions continue to supplant one another from year to year in a sped-up acceleration of inventions coupled with the planned obsolescence of tablets and laptops? Several questions arise: what happens to the memory of past works if their conservation becomes uncertain? And, when a work is transposed from one medium to another, take a comic strip for example, does its readability as well as its comic charge remain intact?

Some claim that paper publication is going to survive on the margins of the Web, but this ignores financial dictates requiring

# WHAT'S SO FUNNY?

significant sales to ensure publishing viability. Are only big names, so-called bestsellers, going to remain? Everyone knows that the whole edifice is necessary to support a few masterpieces. In other words, avant-garde dry runs and stammering discourse are sometimes precursors to great works. If big hits are vital for publishers, the most enlightened among them are well aware that they must take the risk of backing innovators. And this is a throw of the dice, a heady game mixing intellection and revolt.

Clownish politicians, soft and flabby caricatures, gradually disappearing magazines of critical satire, political content shrinking in stand-up comedy: does all this mean that the era is turning its back on incisive criticism? To be sure, cancel culture has brought a new menace to freedom of speech in any venue. Critical humour must reinvent itself.

But let's look at the positive effects of all this development, not to say technological revolution. Internet fosters incredible dialogue, encouraging exchanges among artists and generating wider audiences: blogs and free-access websites are spreading creative works, far beyond territorial borders. Many artists from emerging countries can now be known to their colleagues and likewise have daily access to creations from so-called advanced countries. This ease in communicating is undoubtedly a great school for freedom of expression. Young artists also benefit from modern technologies: they can reach the public more directly. And what about AI in this maelstrom? Will this parrot of cultures be able to speak the subtle language of critical humour, without falling into platitude? And, by the way, is AI even capable of humour?

Satirical websites are now readily available across the globe, for better and for worse. Better, the possibility for readers in third-world countries or under authoritarian rule to access critical humour; worse, that narrow-minded audiences can thus be scandalized by irreverent forms of humour. With the explosive effects we have seen in recent years.

Humorous artists express themselves in extreme language, on a fine line where in principle, everything can be said, because that is where the funny, the comic is found. But often it happens that they are playing with fire. Caricaturists, stage and screen comedians: they are in the line of fire.

Moreover, let us mention that contemporary dramatic events also provoke vivid reactions stirring the critical fiber: just think of

COVID 19, starting in March 2020 or the Ukraine war, beginning in March 2022, or the war between Israel and Hamas beginning in October 2023, and all the representations they have generated. In addition, repeated left-wing assaults through social networks but, mainly, attacks by new right-wing and far-right movements - like Web police - on comedians and cartoonists with whom they disagree are generating resurgent pride among the creators of humour. The freedom of expression we have struggled so hard to acquire has suddenly jumped out at us after being threatened.

The Web, this great unknown, is opening its arms to us. It's as if nothing really connects this form of media to the previous ones, and that it now has to perfect its skills. Who knows if new generations, their eyes riveted on cell phones and tablets while waiting to be hooked up directly, who knows, will find new comic languages. Let us wager they will use the same humorous processes as their ancestors!

# BIBLIOGRAPHY

## "General"

Alexandre, Arsène (1892). *L'art du rire et de la caricature*, Paris, Impressions réunies.

Attardo, Salvatore (1994). *Linguistic Theories of Humor*, New York, Mouton de Gruyter.

---------------------- (2014). *Encyclopedia of Humor Studies*, Thousand Oaks (Calif.), Sage Publ.

Baudelaire, Charles (1846–1864). *Curiosités Esthétiques*, Paris, Hermann, 1968.

Bakhtine, Mikhaïl (1968). *Rabelais and His World*, trans. Hélène Iswolsky, Cambridge, MA, MIT Press.

Bergson, Henri (1900). *Laughter: An Essay on the Meaning of the Comic*, New York, Macmillan and Co., 1911.

Bornemann, Bernd (dir.), Roy Claude, Searle, Ronald (1974). *La caricature, Art et manifeste*, Genève, Skira.

Canova, Marie-Claude (1993). *La comédie*, Paris, Hachette (=Contours littéraires).

Chapman, Anthony J. and Foot, Hugh C. (2017), *Humour and Laughter*, Piscataway (NJ), Transaction Publisher.

Critchley, Simon (2004). *De l'humour*, Paris, Kimé.

Dewey, Donald (2015). *The Art of Ill Will. The Story of American Political Cartoons*, New York Univ. Press.

Escarpit, Robert (1960). *L'humour*, Paris, Presses Universitaires de France (=Que sais-Je?).

Falardeau, Mira (1977). *L'humour visuel. Histoire et technique*, Québec, Les Presses de l'Université Laval (=Cahier de communication graphique, 5)

Ford, Thomas E. and Martin, Rod A. (2018), *The Psychology of Humor*, Amsterdam, Elsevier Inc.

## WHAT'S SO FUNNY?

Freud, Sigmund (1905). *Der Witz und seine Beziehung zum Unbewussten*, Leipzig: Deuticke. (1960) *Jokes and Their Relation to the Unconscious*, New-York, Norton.

Goatly, Andrew (2012). *Meaning and Humour*, New York, Cambridge University Press.

Gepner, Corrina (2001). *Comédie et comique*, Paris, Ellipses (=40/4)

Geyssant, Aline, Guteville, Nicole et Razack, Asifa (dir.) (2000). *Le comique*, Paris, Ellipses.

Gombrich, Ernst (1960). *Art and Illusion. A Study in the Psychology of Pictorial Representation*. London: Phaidon.

Hoffman, Werner, (1957). *Caricature from Vinci to Picasso*, New York: Crown Publ.

Horn, Maurice (1979), *The World Encyclopedia of Comics*, New York, Chelsea House.

Lipovetsky, Gilles (1995) (1983). *The Ephemeral Era*, Baltimore (Md.) Johns Hopkins Univ. Press. *L'ère du vide. Essais sur l'individualisme contemporain*, Paris, Gallimard.

Martin, Rod A. (2006), *The Psychology of Humor*, Cambridge (Mass.), Academic Press.

Machovec, Frank J. (2012). *Humor. Theory, History, Applications*, Bloomington (In.), iUniverse.

McCloud, Scott (2000). *Reinventing Comics*, New York, Harper Collins Publ.

Melchior-Bonnet, Sabine (2021). *Le rire des femmes*, Paris, PUF.

Melot, Michet (1975). *L'œil qui rit. Le pouvoir comique des images*, Fribourg, L'Office du livre.

Minois, Georges (2000). *Histoire du rire et de la dérision*, Paris, Fayard.

Moliterni, Claude, Mellot, Philippe, Denni, Michel (1996). *Les aventures de la BD*, Paris, Gallimard (=Découvertes Gallimard).

Nietzche, Friedrich (1882) (1974). *The Gay Science*, trad. from *Die fröhliche Wissenschaft*, New York, Penguin (= Vintage).

Pearson, Hesketh (1963). *Bernard Shaw: His Life and Personality*, Atheneum Press.

Pollock, Jonathan (2001). *Qu'est-ce que l'humour?* Paris, Klincksieck.

Piaget, Jean (1967). *Six Psychological Studies*, New York, Penguin (= Vintage).

Sangsue, Daniel (1994). *La parodie*, Paris, Hachette.

Schaeffer, Neil (1981). *The Art of Laughter*, New York, Columbia University Press.

Sibony, Daniel (2010). *Le sens du rire et de l'humour*, Paris, Odile Jacob.

Simpson, Paul (2003). *On the Discourse of Satire*, Philadelphia, John Benjamins Publ.

160

# MIRA FALARDEAU

Stefiik, Mark J. (1997). *Archetypes, Myths and Metaphors*, Cambridge (Ma): MIT Press.

Victorofff, David (1953). *Le rire et le risible*, Paris, Presses Universitaires de France.

## "Articles, chapters and websites"

Ballagriga, Alain (2006). « Aspects du rire rituel en Grèce antique », *Humoresques*. 24. 23–34.

Boskin, J. (1990). « American Political Humor: Touchables and Taboos », *International Political Science Review*, 11(4), 473–482 – Idem pour (Falardeau (1976) and (2000) and all others (Kotthoff, LeGoff, Meyer, Suls, Veatch, Yus, Zillman

Devaux, Alexandre (2006). « Hara-Kiri mensuel : le berceau de l'humour bête et méchant », *Humoresques*. 23. 101–119.

Dynel, Martha (2008). 'Introduction to Special Issue on Humor: a Modest Attempt at Presenting Contemporary Linguistic Approaches to Humor Studies", *Lodz Papers in Pragmatics* 4.1/ *Special Issue on Humor*. 1–12.

Falardeau, Mira (1978). *L'humour visuel; un modèle d'analyse visuelle des images comiques*, École des gradués, Faculté des Lettres, Université Laval, Service des thèses.

-------------- (1976). « Pour une analyse de l'image comique », *Communication/ Information*, vol. III. 3, p. 21–53.

------------(2000). « La BD française est née au Canada en 1904 », *Communication et Langages*, no 126, p. 23–47.

Eco, Umberto (1970). « Sémiologie des messages visuels », *Communications*, L'analyse des images. 15. 11–52.

Feuerhahn, Nelly (2006). « Sourire vertical, rire et ruse au féminin. Déméter et Amaterasu », *Humoresques*. 24. 152–161.

Friedemann, Joë (1998). « Le rire dans Notre-Dame de Paris : de la fête des fous à la damnation », *Humoresques*. 9. 65–77.

Gerbet website, Thomas (2021). Ici Radio-Canada web site, Sep 7 2021

Kotthoff, Helga (2006). "Gender and Humor: The State of the Art", *Journal of Pragmatics*, vol. 38, no 1, Jan. 2006, p. 4–25.

Kossaifi, Christine (2006). « Le rire de Pan entre mythe et psychanalyse », *Humoresques*. 24. 36–54.

Kutz-Flamenbaum, R.V. (2014). "Humor and Social Movements", *Sociology Compass*, 3(8), p. 294- 304.

LeGoff, Jacques (1989). « Rire au Moyen Âge », *Les cahiers de recherche historique* (en ligne). 3. http//ccrh.revues.org/2910 consulté en janvier 2015.

## WHAT'S SO FUNNY?

Meyer, J.C. (2000). "Humor as a Double-Edged Sword: Four Functions of Humor in Communication", *Communication Theory*, 10(3), p. 310–331.

Morin, Violette (1966). « L'histoire drôle », *Communications*. 8. 102–131.

---(1970). « Le dessin humoristique », *Communications*. 15. 110–131.

Morton, Victor (2019). "Antonio Moreira Antunes, New York Times cartoonist, exhibited anti-Semitic work in 1983", *Washington Post*, April 28, 2019.

Noguez, Dominique (1974). « Petite rhétorique de poche, pour servir à la lecture des dessins dits « d'humour », *Revue d'esthétique*, Spécial : L'art de masse n'existe pas, 3–4. 106–137.

Platow, M.J., Haslam, A.S., Both, A., Chew, I., Cuddon, M., Goharpey, N., Maurer, J., Rosini, S., Tsekouras, A., M.Grace, D. (2005). "It's not funny if they're laughing: Selfcategorization, social influence, and responses to canned laughter", *Journal of Experimental Social Psychology*, 41, 542–550.

Raskin, V. (1979). "Semantic Mechanisms of Humor", *Annual Meeting of the Berkeley Linguistics Society*, vol. 5, 1979, p. 325–335.

Rivoli-Ruspoli, Dominique (2006). « Quand les déesses rient », *Humoresques*. 24. 148–151.

Roy, Samantha (2011). *Le grotesque dans les fabliaux érotiques : figure féminine et poétique du rire populaire*, Maîtrise en études littéraires, UQTR.

Sagnard, Arnaud (2021). « Dave Chappelle, mauvais esprit », *L'OBS,* no 2978, 11–18–2021.

Sarrazin, Bernard (1998), Compte-rendu de Horowitz, Jeannine et Menache, Sophia (1994). *L'humour en chaire. Le rire dans l'Église médiévale*, Genève, Labor Fides. *Humoresques,* no 9, 121–126.

Suls, J.M. (1972). "A Two-Stage Model for the Appreciation of Jokes and Cartoons: An Information-Processing Analysis", in J.H. Goldstein et P.E. Mcghee, *The Psychology of Humor: Theoretical Perspectives and Empirical Issues,* New York: Academic Press, p.81- 100.

Veatch, T.C. (1998). "A Theory of Humor", *Humor: International Journal of Humor Research*, 11(2), p. 161–216.

Yus, Franscisco, (2003). "Humor and the Search of Relevance", *Journal of Pragmatics*, vol. 35, no 9, Sep. 2003, p. 1295–1331.

Zillman, Dolf (1983) "Disparagement Humor", in: McGhee, P.E. Goldstein, J.H. (eds), *Handbook of Humor Research*, Springer, New York, p. 85–107.

## "Extracts"

Apollinaire, Guillaume, *Calligrammes, Poems of Peace and War* (1918), The Public Domain Review, online.

Beckett, Samuel (1948) (2011). *Waiting for Godot,* New York, Grove Press.

Breton, André (1939) (2001). *The Anthology of Black Humor (Anthologie de l'humour noir)*, San Francisco (Calif.), City Lights Publishers.

Carroll, Lewis (1865) (1993), *Alice's Adventures in Wonderland*, New York, Dover Publications.

Doyle, Conan (1913). *How it Happened, Tales of Twilight and the Unseen*, London, Alma Books.

Eco, Umberto (1983) (2016). *The Name of the Rose (Il nome della rosa)*, London, Minerva.

Hollander, Nicole (1981). *"That woman must be on drugs"*, New York, St-Martin's Press.

Leacock, Stephen (circa 1910) (1993). *My Financial Carrer and Other Folies*, Toronto, Penguin Random House (=New Canadian Library)

Molière (1669) (1997). *Tartuffe: A Comedy in Five Acts*, Orlando (Fl.), Harbour Brace and Company.

Molière (1673) (1939). *The Imaginary Invalid (Le malade imaginaire)*, Chicago, Dramatic Publishing.

Rabelais, François (1534–1552) (2006). *Gargantua and Pantagruel*, London, Penguin Classics.

Rostand, Edmond (1897) (2006). *Cyrano de Bergerac*, London, Penguin Classics.

Shakespeare, William (1590) (2014). *The Taming of the Shrew*, New York, Simon & Schuster.

Shakespeare, William (1600). *The Second Part of King Henry IV*, Folger Shakespeare Library.

Shakespeare, William (1602). *The Merry Wives of Windsor*, Folger Shakespeare Library.

# INDEX

## A

Accumulation: humour through repetition and gradation, 78, 81

Advertising: use of humour to captivate audiences, 12, 15

Alexamenos graffito: early humorous graffiti mocking Christianity, 6

Amaterasu (Japanese goddess): humour in Japanese mythology, 3

Anthropomorphism: human traits in animals for humour, 88, 99

Aristophanes:
The *Assemblywomen*: gender and politics satire, 5, 6
The *Birds*: critique of utopian ideals, 5
The *Clouds*: parody of philosophers, 5
The *Frogs*: commentary on art and society, 5
The Wasps: satire of legal systems, 5

Aristotle:
Theory of comedy and defect as humour, 5
Influence on comic arts in ancient Greece, 5, 17

Attardo, Salvatore: contributions to humour theory, 17

## B

Bakhtin, Mikhail: concept of carnival and the carnivalesque, 19

Ballagrida, André: studies on laughter in rituals, 3, 5

Baubô: comic relief in mythological rituals, 3

Baudelaire, Charles: analysis of Goya's grotesque humour, 22

Bernini, Gian Lorenzo:
Caricature sketches for the court of Louis XIV, 14
Techniques in distortion of individual features, 14

Black bile: melancholia in humour theory, 17

# INDEX

Bosch, Hieronymus:
 Grotesque figures in *The Garden of Earthly Delights*, 11
 Influence on Renaissance caricatures, 11
Buffoonery: medieval humour in fairs and festivals, 8, 10

## C

Cancel culture and humour: impact on modern comedy, 54, 57
Caricature:
 Early examples in Renaissance art, 6, 14
 Evolution from private to public humour, 16, 22
 Manuals by Francis Grose and Mary Darly, 16
Carracci brothers: Renaissance caricature artists, 14
Cartoons: history from early satire to modern media, 6, 11, 20
Carnival: origins in Dionysian festivals and its comic elements, 19, 20
Choleric temperament: role in humour theories, 5
Classical Greece:
 Birth of democratic humour, 3, 5
 Satirical commentary in Greek theatre, 5
Commedia dell'arte:
 Improvisation and masks in humour, 11, 12

Influence on later European comedy, 11
Contrast: as a tool for creating humour, 59, 64

## D

Dionysian festivals:
 Humour and excess in ancient Greece, 4, 5
 Connection to modern carnivals, 4
Double meaning: visual and verbal techniques in humour, 107, 112
Dürer, Albrecht:
 Analysis of human proportions for humour, 13, 16
 Contribution to grotesque art, 13, 16

## E

Elizabethan theatre:
 Role of humour in Shakespeare's works, 12
 Continuation of Greek and Roman comic traditions, 12
Escarpit, Robert: commentary on the difficulty of defining humour, 17
Exaggeration:
 Stylistic process amplifying absurdity, 18, 20
 Historical examples from masks to caricature, 19

## F

Fabliaux:
 Medieval comic poetry mocking societal norms, 9

166

# INDEX

Performed by troubadours, 9

Farce:
Development from medieval fairs to theatre, 8, 11
Influence on Molière's comedic style, 11

Ferzat, Ali: Syrian cartoonist punished for political satire, 3

Freedom of expression:
Role of humour in challenging authority, 1, 12, 54
Historical and modern examples, 1, 54

G

Galen: development of the four temperaments, 5

Gargoyles:
Grotesque figures in medieval architecture, 9
Link to caricature, 9
Goya, Francisco de:
Integration of grotesque and humour, 22
Commentary on society through satire, 22
Gradation: humour through escalating patterns, 78, 84
Grose, Francis:
Author of caricature manual *Rules for Drawing Caricaturas*, 16

H

Hippocrates:
Theory of humours and their role in laughter, 5

Influence on medical and comedic thought, 5

Hogarth, William:
*Characters and Caricatures*: boundaries of realism and satire, 21
Social commentary through exaggerated portraits, 21

Homer:
Humour in *The Iliad* and *The Odyssey*, 3
Influence on comic storytelling, 3

Humours (bodily):
Historical theories linking them to temperament, 5, 17

I

Ideograms: visual simplification in humour, 47

Irony:
Use in contrast and inversion, 59, 64
Examples from literature and visual arts, 64

J

Jonson, Ben:
*Every Man in His Humor*: role of jesters, 17
Intersection of humour and madness, 17

L

Leonardo da Vinci:
Studies of grotesque heads, 14, 20

# INDEX

Exploration of beauty and distortion, 14, 20

Lipovetsky, Gilles: concept of the "humorous society," 12

**M**

Masks:
Use in ancient theatre and carnivals, 5, 19
Role in commedia dell'arte and identity, 12

Melancholy:
Connection to humour in artistic traditions, 17
Explored in visual and literary works, 17

Metaphor and metonymy:
Techniques in visual and textual humour, 122, 136

Molière:
*The Miser:* satire of greed, 12
*The Imaginary Invalid:* critique of medicine, 12
*Amphitryon:* irony and disguise, 12

Monkeys: debated ability to laugh, 9

**N**

Nonsense:
Use in absurd humour, 114
Visual and verbal examples, 114

**P**

Parody:
Humour in media and literature, 54
Role in mediatization of humour, 54

Picture interpretation:
Evolution of techniques in visual humour, 10, 20

Plautus:
Roman comedy and its legacy, 5, 12

Preachers:
Use of humour in medieval sermons, 9

**R**

Rabelais, François:
*Gargantua:* satire of societal excess, 11
*Pantagruel:* exploration of bawdy humour, 11
Influence on Renaissance comedy, 11

Repetition:
Patterns as a humour technique, 78
Examples in text and performance, 78

Renaissance art: grotesque and its comic influence, 11

Rowlandson, Thomas:
Eccentric characters and social critique, 22

**S**

Satirical newspapers: growth during the 19th century, 22

Satyrs: comic figures in ancient rituals, 5

Shakespeare, William:
*Much Ado About Nothing:* romantic and ridiculous humour, 12
*Twelfth Night:* comedy of excess, 17

# INDEX

*The Taming of the Shrew:*
  gender roles and satire, 12
Simplification:
Visual techniques in humour,
  30, 40
Socrates: mocked in
  Aristophanes' *The Clouds*,
  5

T
Terence:
  Roman comedy traditions, 5
  Legacy in theatrical humour,
  5
Thesmophories:
  Greek festivals with comic
  and ribald rituals, 3

Troubadours:
  Performers of medieval
  comic poetry, 9

V
Visual double meaning:
  techniques in cartoons and
  caricatures, 112
Visual humour:
  Development across media,
  12, 19, 110

W
Word games:
  Verbal techniques in humour,
  103, 105